IMAGES OF WAR

AXIS TANKS OF THE SECOND WORLD WAR

RARE PHOTOGRAPHS FROM WARTIME ARCHIVES

Michael Green

Pen & Sword
MILITARY

First published in Great Britain in 2017 by
PEN & SWORD MILITARY
An imprint of
Pen & Sword Books Ltd
47 Church Street
Barnsley
South Yorkshire
S70 2AS

ISBN 978-1-47388-700-8

Typeset by Concept, Huddersfield, West Yorkshire HD4 5JL.
Printed and bound in India by Replika Press Pvt. Ltd.

Pen & Sword Books Ltd incorporates the imprints of Pen & Sword Archaeology, Atlas, Aviation, Battleground, Discovery, Family History, History, Maritime, Military, Naval, Politics, Railways, Select, Social History, Transport, True Crime, and Claymore Press, Frontline Books, Leo Cooper, Praetorian Press, Remember When, Seaforth Publishing and Wharncliffe.

For a complete list of Pen & Sword titles please contact
PEN & SWORD BOOKS LIMITED
47 Church Street, Barnsley, South Yorkshire S70 2AS, England
E-mail: enquiries@pen-and-sword.co.uk
Website: www.pen-and-sword.co.uk

Contents

Dedication

The author would like to dedicate this book to
fellow tank buff Ian Wilcox for all his help with this title and others.

Foreword

Michael Green's comparative study of Axis tanks demonstrates well the unique military situations of the three largest nations starting the Second World War. Germany, Japan and Italy had conducted their rearmament programmes in advance of their opponents and enjoyed certain advantages for a limited period of time. However, upon closer examination each encountered fatal weaknesses, even though the war continued for several years.

Japan and Italy both began their rearmament programmes early in the 1930s, and the development of their respective tank arms demonstrated a great deal of progress over the crude tanks of the First World War. In particular, lighter and handier machines with modern diesel and gasoline engines incorporating automotive advances in suspensions and more effective weapons served very well in the incipient warfare of the 1930s. However, the costs of the wars of the 1930s inhibited further progress to a considerable extent.

Italian forces participated in General Franco's eventual victory of his Nationalist forces in the Spanish Civil War. Hundreds of light tanks, armoured cars and aircraft were sent with their own forces and most of the equipment was lost, worn out or left behind for the use of their Spanish compatriots. On the ground, Italian forces eventually demonstrated a form of mechanized warfare novel for the time, emphasizing mass and rapid movements to exploit enemy dispositions and affect a pursuit. Although doctrine and organization for their armoured division showed evident promise, the general staff did not allocate resources for the medium and heavy tanks it required and in 1940 most armoured units were of the paper form.

Japanese tanks proved useful in their expansion into China, and in the opening months of the Pacific War, the Japanese army put them into operation in their rapid conquest of Dutch and British colonies. Frequently they appeared in campaigns where the Allies had judged armour unsuitable for employment, much to their surprise and demise. On the other hand, the brief combat encounters with tanks of the Soviet Union during border conflicts in Manchuria demonstrated that Japanese armour remained demonstrably inferior.

In the end, only Germany of all the Axis powers had the economic, industrial and technological bases for advanced tank development. Despite its limited experimentation with tanks before the Nazi seizure of power, the German army had sound doctrine for manoeuvre warfare using motorized troops, and German industry overcame initial handicaps to begin production of two medium tank designs by 1938 that greatly facilitated success in battle in the opening years of the war. Ironically, these tanks displayed neither the best armament nor armour nor speed among their contemporaries. However, what they did incorporate in their designs proved decisive: a three-man turret and a radio. They also were of sufficient size that their weapons and armour could be augmented as the gun/armour race of the war evolved.

The German tankers of 1940–41 encountered tough opponents in those years mounted in British Matilda, French Char B or Russian T-34 tanks. They managed to outfight them thanks to superior organization and tactics, aided by the fact that the vehicle commander had no duties serving the gun and he had radio contact with all his tanks and his higher commander.

By the end of 1942, however, the Axis reached the limits of their initial advantages and no new tanks, be they Panthers or Tigers, could counter the crushing superiority of the three major Allied powers that caught up with and surpassed them in technology and organization.

Kenneth W. Estes, PhD.
Lieutenant Colonel, US Marine Corps
Author, *Marines Under Armor*

Acknowledgments

As with any published work, authors must depend on a great many people for assistance. These included, over many years, my fellow author and long-time mentor the late Richard Hunnicutt. Other friends who kindly supplied pictures for this work are credited in the captions.

Both the paid and volunteer staff of the now-closed Patton Museum of Armor and Cavalry provided the author with a great deal of assistance over many years. For the sake of brevity all images from the former Patton Museum of Cavalry and Armor will be credited to the 'Patton Museum'.

I am also indebted to David Fletcher, fellow author and the long-time former librarian at the Tank Museum located in Bovington, England. He has greatly assisted the author in locating photographs for many of his books. All images from the Tank Museum in Bovington will be credited to just the 'Tank Museum' for brevity.

Notes to the Reader

1. Due to the size and format restrictions imposed by the publisher on this series of books the author will concentrate on the gun tank versions of the vehicles described in the text. Those tanks converted to support-based versions such as self-propelled artillery or anti-aircraft vehicles will be covered in a subsequent title.
2. Prior to the Second World War and during the conflict armies generally classified their tanks as light, medium or heavy, based on the weight of the tank. The weight classifications of what constituted the breakdown between the different types of tank varied from one country to another, with one army's heavy tank being another's medium tank, for example.
3. The quality of some images in this book is rather substandard. However, they have been included due to the historical rarity of the subject pictured.
4. Both the Waffen SS and the Luftwaffe field divisions employed tanks during the Second World War. For the sake of brevity the author will put these under the umbrella term of 'German army' in this work.

Chapter One

Light Tanks

In the 1920s, the German army began thinking about the need for tanks. Undecided at that time was whether light or medium tanks were a better choice. Some thought that large numbers of small and cheap light tanks could overwhelm an opposing enemy by sheer force of numbers. In 1930 a German army officer wrote that the proposed light tanks should be supported in battle by a smaller number of better-armed and armoured medium tanks.

Many in the German army favoured light tanks due to the realistic view that German industry then lacked the experience and infrastructure to design and build the required number of medium tanks. It was eventually decided to go ahead with the production of light tanks as they could be built cheaply and quickly in large numbers for equipping the new Panzer divisions. The first three divisions were formed in 1935, with twenty-one being in existence by the summer of 1941.

A Light Tank Appears

In 1933, the German army laid out the requirements for a light tank. The new light tank was to be crewed by two men: the tank commander in the turret, which was armed with two machine guns, and the driver in the hull. The machine-gun armament chosen for the tank was fairly standard armament on light tanks of that time.

A tank turret in German is referred to as a *Turm*, completed or uncompleted. The uncompleted hull of a tank was referred to as the *Wanne*. Once completed it becomes known as a *Fahrgestell* (complete chassis).

Krupp AG was selected to begin work on the chassis of the new light tank and Daimler-Benz AG the upper hull (also known as the superstructure) and turret. In the German language the superstructure or superstructure and turret of a tank are referred to as the *Aufbau*. Modern tanks have no upper hull/superstructure, only a hull and a turret.

Full-scale production of the new light tank for the German army began in July 1934. It was designated the Pz.Kpfw.I Ausf. A. The abbreviation Pz.Kpfw. stands for *Panzer-kampfwagen*, which translates into English as armoured fighting vehicle. For the sake of brevity, throughout the remainder of the text the author will employ the word 'Panzer' in lieu of Pz.Kpfw.

The abbreviation 'Ausf.' is for the German word *Ausführung* and refers to a specific version of a vehicle, with the letter following representing a model improvement in alphabetical sequence. The Panzer I series was also assigned the ordnance inventory number 101. In German documents a vehicle's ordnance inventory number is prefixed by the abbreviation Sd.Kfz. which stands for *Sonderkraftfahrzeug* or special-purpose motor vehicle.

Panzer I Background

Production of the approximately 12,000lb Panzer I Ausf. A continued till 1936, with a total of 818 units completed. To meet the number of light tanks required by the German army, a number of different manufacturers were involved in the programme. The replacement for the Panzer I Ausf. A was an improved heavier and longer model labelled the Panzer I Ausf. B. A total of 675 units were built between 1935 and 1937 of the approximately 13,000lb tank.

Both models of the Panzer I series had a maximum armour thickness of 13mm, proof against machine-gun fire only. They had a top speed on level roads of approximately 23mph. The Panzer I Ausf. A was powered by a Krupp air-cooled gasoline engine, which proved underpowered in service.

The Panzer I Ausf. B was provided with a far superior Maybach liquid-cooled gasoline engine. All subsequent German-designed and built tanks would be powered by Maybach liquid-cooled rear hull-mounted gasoline engines.

Into Combat

By 1936, some in the German army began to question the combat usefulness of the Panzer I. Despite these doubts, Adolf Hitler committed 180 of them to take part in the Spanish Civil War (1936–39). Their combat debut was not impressive as the Soviet army light tanks supplied to the other side in the conflict were better armed and armoured than the German light tanks.

During the German military invasion of Poland in September 1939 a total of 1,445 units of the Panzer I were committed to battle. Of that number, eighty-nine were lost in combat. Despite the successful conclusion of the German campaign in Poland, which took only thirty days, it was clear to all that the Panzer I was already obsolete. Despite their poor showing in Poland, 523 units of the Panzer I were committed to the invasion of France and the Low Countries in June 1940 as nothing else was then available.

Two German army divisions arrived in North Africa in February 1942. They were equipped with approximately 150 tanks, of which 89 were the Panzer I series. From a translated German army report appears this extract on what they thought of the Panzer I in North Africa: 'Panzerkampfwagen I is considered too weak and slow, breaking down frequently.'

For the invasion of the Soviet Union in June 1941 the German army amassed a total of 3,332 tanks, of which 410 were the Panzer I Ausf. B. The Ausf. A had already been withdrawn from front-line service and relegated to other roles. The majority of Panzer I Ausf. Bs that took part in the opening stages of the Eastern Front campaign were already assigned secondary roles, such as command and control vehicles.

Panzer I Series Dead Ends

In 1939, the German army decided that it required a high-speed and up-armoured version of the Panzer I series for the reconnaissance role. It therefore awarded Krauss-Maffei a contract to design and build a suitable chassis and Daimler-Benz a contract to build the superstructure and turret. The final product was designated as the Panzer I Ausf. C. It had a top speed on level roads of 50mph.

Armed with a 20mm main gun and a machine gun, the maximum armour thickness of the Panzer I Ausf. C was 30mm. Only forty units of the approximately 18,000lb vehicle were built in 1942. Two were tested on the Eastern Front in 1943. The test results must not have been positive enough to warrant continued production of such a specialized vehicle and all were consigned to secondary duties as training vehicles.

Also ordered in 1939 by the German army was a two-man version of the Panzer I series intended as an infantry support tank. It was designated the Panzer I Ausf. F and rode on the suspension system developed for the Panzer I Ausf. C. The approximately 40,000lb vehicle had a maximum armour thickness of 80mm and was armed with two machine guns. Top speed on level roads was 15mph. Only thirty units were built in 1942 before the decision was made to end production.

Panzer II

Concerns about production delays with its much-anticipated new medium tanks led the German army to order a new, larger and better-armed light tank in 1934 as a stop-gap measure. It was designated the Panzer II. *Maschinenfabrik Augsburg Nürnberg* (MAN) had been assigned the job of designing the chassis of the Panzer II and Daimler-Benz the superstructure and turret. Western Allied wartime reports referred to the Panzer II as the 'Mark II'.

Prior to placing the Panzer II into full production, a number of trial or developmental models were constructed in varying numbers between 1935 and early 1937. They were intended to perfect the vehicle's design, especially the suspension system. The Panzer II series was assigned the ordnance inventory number 121.

The Panzer II was operated by three men and armed with a 20mm gun and a coaxial machine gun. The tank's original 20mm gun was designated as the 2cm KwK 30. The letter prefix KwK is a German abbreviation for *Kampfwagenkanone* or tank gun. A 1939 German army training manual describes the manner of firing the

20mm gun on the Panzer II: 'Short bursts of two to three rounds is the normal method of engaging targets from fire positions or on the move.'

The same 1939 training manual goes on to discuss the choice of targets and their suggested engagement ranges for the Panzer II tank crew: 'Enemy tanks should be engaged from static fire positions at a range of 600 metres [660 yards]. The gun can also be used against enemy anti-tank guns at ranges of 500 metres [550 yards], but only if it is impossible to outflank the enemy and engage it with machine guns.'

Production

The first full-scale production model of the Panzer II series came off the assembly line in July 1937 and was designated the Panzer II Ausf. A. It was followed by the very similar Ausf. B and Ausf. C versions. Approximately 1,100 units of the first three full-scale production models of the Panzer II were completed by April 1940. The last model of the Panzer II series built in large numbers and very similar in appearance to the earlier models was the Ausf. F with 524 built between 1941 and 1942.

In between the Panzer II Ausf. C and Ausf. F models were the Ausf. D and Ausf. E versions. Only forty units were built from May 1938 to August 1939 of the two nearly identical vehicles. They retained the standard turret of the Panzer II series but with an entirely new chassis riding on a torsion bar suspension system.

Intended as dedicated reconnaissance vehicles, the Panzer II Ausf. E and Ausf. F models had a maximum speed on level roads of 34mph. By comparison, the other models of the Panzer II series could only muster a top speed of 24mph. The Panzer II Ausf. E and Ausf. F models would see use during the invasion of Poland but were then pulled from service and converted for another role.

Like the Panzer I, the Panzer II series proved to be under-armoured and under-gunned on the battlefield. Following the Polish campaign the various models of the tank were up-armoured with factory-applied 20mm frontal add-on armour kits. Maximum base armour on the first three production models of the Panzer II series was only 15mm. The Panzer II Ausf. F had a maximum base armour of 30mm and weighed approximately 21,000lb.

Combat

The Panzer II series would take part in the invasion of France, the fighting in North Africa and the early stages of the invasion of the Soviet Union. Efforts to up-arm the Panzer II series were never realized. They were only suitable for the reconnaissance role by 1940. This role is described in a May 1943 Allied bulletin. Within it appears a summarized description of the employment of the Panzer II in offensive operations and some extracts of that report follow:

The light tank [Panzer II] patrol advances rapidly from one observation post to the next. Making use at first of roads and paths, but later, as it approaches hostile forces, using all available cover. When approaching villages, woods, or defiles, the patrol leaves the road in sufficient time to upset the opposition's aimed anti-tank-fire calculations … The German patrol commander makes a rapid estimate of our position and tries to attack and overrun us if he thinks that we are weak. If such a move does not seem advisable, he attempts to discover the type and strength of the opposition encountered without becoming involved in combat.

The Panzer II series also performed other battlefield roles besides reconnaissance. Some were employed as command and control vehicles in support of German army medium tank units. This is seen in a passage from a July 1942 US army publication on the fighting in North Africa: 'The commander of the [German army] unit was in a Mark II tank. He kept 60 to 80 yards behind the line, cruising backwards and forwards, and his radio control appeared to work very well. There was another Mark II apparently carrying a FOOC (Forward Observation Officer Command).'

Production of the Panzer II Ausf. F concluded in December 1942. A great many units of the Panzer II series would be eventually rebuilt and converted for other roles including self-propelled artillery pieces and anti-tank vehicles.

Panzer II Design Dead End

In a dilution of industrial effort a number of experimental test models considered part of the Panzer II series were designed and built in very small numbers starting in April 1941. The final result of this developmental work resulted in the production of a dedicated high-speed reconnaissance version designated the Panzer II Ausf. L. It was assigned the ordnance inventory number 123 and the official nickname *Luchs* (Lynx).

Between September 1943 and January 1944 approximately 100 units of the *Luchs* were constructed by MAN out of an initial order for 800 units. Like the Panzer II Ausf. D and Ausf. E, the *Luchs* rode on a torsion bar suspension system. The four-man vehicle was armed with a 20mm gun designated the 2cm KwK 38 and a coaxial machine gun. It was also fitted with long-distance radios.

It was intended that later-production units of the approximately 29,000lb *Luchs* be armed with a 50mm gun. As production was cancelled early on, this up-arming never took place. Maximum armour protection on the vehicle was 30mm. It had a top speed on level roads of almost 38mph.

Czech Light Tanks

In the years leading up to the Second World War, German industry was finding it extremely difficult to build enough tanks to equip all the newly-formed Panzer divisions. This problem was partially solved by the German annexation of Czechoslovakia on 15 March 1939. This act of political aggression, backed up by the implied threat of a military invasion, led the German army to acquire the entire inventory of weapons and equipment belonging to the abruptly-disbanded Czech army.

Among the many vehicles acquired by the German army were 427 units of a light tank that had been designated the LT vz 35 by the Czech army. Some 218 were impressed into German army service and re-designated the Panzer 35(t). The letter suffix 't' stood for Czech. The LT vz 35 would also serve in small numbers with some of Germany's wartime allies' armies. These would include the Bulgarian, Romanian and Slovakian armies.

The approximately 23,000lb Panzer 35(t) had a crew of four in German army service and was armed with a 37mm main gun plus two machine guns. Maximum armour protection on the tank was 35mm thick. Powered by a liquid-cooled gasoline engine, the Panzer 35(t) had a top speed on level roads of approximately 25mph. It would see service with the German army from the invasion of Poland through to the end of 1941 on the Eastern Front.

A Second Czech Tank in German Service
Upon taking over the Czech armament factory of CKD in May 1941, the German army came upon an unknown light tank designated the LT vz 38. Of this model, 150 had been ordered by the Czech army but none had been delivered prior to the German takeover. Upon testing the first nine off the factory floor the German army was very impressed, so much so that they ordered the tank into full-scale production for themselves and designated it the Panzer 38(t).

Between 1939 and 1942, a total of 1,396 units of the Panzer 38(t) were built for the German army in a series of slightly different models. The Panzer 38(t) had the same crew complement and armament array as the Panzer 35(t). Maximum armour thickness on the approximately 21,000lb vehicle was 25mm. The Panzer divisions that were issued the Panzer 38(t) considered it, as with the Panzer 35(t), superior to their own light tanks in firepower and mobility as well as overall reliability.

As with the Panzer 35(t), the Panzer 38(t) would serve with the German army from Poland up through to the initial stages of the invasion of the Soviet Union. The Red Army T-34 medium tank and the KV-1 heavy quickly rendered them useless on the battlefield and hastened their departure from front-line service by 1942. Besides the German army, the gasoline-engine-powered Panzer 38(t) would be employed in relatively small numbers by the Slovakian, Hungarian, Bulgarian and Romanian armies.

Panzer 38(t) Variants
There were two specialized reconnaissance models of the Panzer 38(t) developed for the German army. The first was designated the Panzer 38(t) nA. It retained the armament array of the Panzer 38(t) in a newly-designed turret. Equipped with a more powerful gasoline engine than that fitted in the Panzer 38(t), it had a maximum speed

on level roads of approximately 40mph. Only five prototypes were built between 1941 and 1943.

The Panzer 38(t) n.A. was followed in 1944 by the production of seventy units of another specialized high-speed reconnaissance model of the Panzer 38(t). It was intended as the replacement for the *Luchs* and was armed with a 20mm gun and a coaxial machine gun in an open-topped turret. The vehicle's official full German designation was *Aufklärer auf Fahrgestell Panzerkampfwagen* 38(t) *mit* 2cm KwK 38. There were plans to arm it with a low-velocity short-barrelled 75mm gun but that never went into production.

Captured Light Tanks

Always short of tanks throughout the Second World War due to the shortcomings of German industry, the German army sometimes pressed captured tanks into service in limited numbers. Typically these vehicles would be confined to performing secondary roles such as internal security or training. The German army referred to these tanks as *Beute Panzerkampfwagen* (Booty Panzers).

Upon its successful conquest of France in the summer of 1941, the German army acquired a large inventory of French army light tanks. As there was a plentiful supply of spare parts available and factories in the country to maintain them, some were modified for German army use as gun-armed tanks. This involved them being re-painted and given German markings. In many cases they were also fitted with a new German-designed vehicle commander's split hatch.

To reflect the change in ownership of these French army light tanks they were assigned new German designations. Examples would include the Renault 35, which became the Panzer 35r 731(f) and the Hotchkiss H-35/38/39 series, which became the Panzer 38H 735(f). The letter suffix 'f' in the vehicle designations represents a French-built vehicle in the German army nomenclature system.

The German army kept the Panzer 35r 731(f) in France as a training and internal vehicle. The Panzer 38H 735(f) would see service with the German army as an internal security vehicle in both occupied Norway and the Balkans. The great majority of the French light tanks were eventually out of German army service by 1944 due to shortages of spare parts and mechanical issues. Some, however, would be passed on to Germany's wartime allies.

There is pictorial evidence showing that stock examples of captured Red Army light tanks, such as the T-26 series, were sometimes employed by German army units on the Eastern Front. To prevent friendly-fire incidents all had oversized German markings painted on both their hulls and turrets. In most cases it can be assumed that these captured enemy tanks were used until they were lost in combat or suffered serious mechanical problems.

Italian Light Tanks

Upon Italy's entry into the Second World War in June 1940, the Italian army had a very mixed bag of tanks in its inventory. This included approximately ninety units of the *Carro d'assalto Fiat 3000 modello* light tank series, shortened to Fiat 3000 for the sake of brevity. They were a modified Italian-built copy of the French army's First World War vintage FT light tank. The Italian version weighed approximately 12,000lb and had a top speed on level roads of 15mph.

The Fiat 3000 series, which consisted of an A and B model, were later respectively designated the L5/21 and the L5/30. The letter prefix 'L' stood for light tank; the number '5' the weight of the tank in tons; and the final two numbers the year the vehicle was introduced into Italian army service. The two-man light tank could be armed with a machine gun or a 37mm main gun. Maximum armour protection for the Fiat 3000 series was 16mm.

New Light Tanks Enter the Inventory

In the late 1920s, the Italian army ordered a single example of the commercially-available British two-man Carden Lloyd VI machine-gun-armed light tank. A popular term for the British vehicle during the day was 'tankette' due to its very small size and light weight of approximately 3,000lb. Maximum armour protection on the vehicle was 9mm thick.

The Italian army ordered twenty-five additional units of the Carden Lloyd VI in 1929 with the last four delivered as kits and constructed in Italy. In Italian army service the vehicle was labelled the *Carro Veloce* (fast tank) 29, which for brevity's sake the author will refer to as the CV-29.

Italian industry continued to improve on the design of the CV-29 and eventually came up with a new larger and heavier two-man turretless machine-gun-armed version. In 1933, the Italian army ordered it into production as the CV-33. It weighed approximately 12,000lb and had a maximum speed on level roads of 26mph. The thickest armour on the two-man vehicle was 9mm.

Progressively improved models in the CV-33 series were designated the CV-35 and CV-38, with the last production unit coming off the assembly line in 1943. The CV-38 was relabelled the *Carro* L3/35 in 1938. In total, some 2,884 units were built in the series. Besides being mechanically unreliable, all proved to be woefully under-armoured and under-gunned when confronted by British army tanks in North Africa.

The intended replacement for the CV-33 through to CV-38 was the two-man *Carro Armato Leggero* (armoured tank, light) L6/40. The approximately 15,000lb vehicle had a turret-mounted 20mm main gun plus machine guns. Maximum armour thickness on the vehicle was 30mm. A total of 402 units of the L6/40 were built between 1941 and 1943. Combat action in North Africa showed that the L6/40 and all the previous models of the CV-33 series were totally obsolete by the standards of the day.

Hungarian Light Tanks

In 1936, the Hungarian army acquired a single example of a Swedish light tank labelled the Landsverk L-60. The three-man tank was armed with a turret-mounted 20mm main gun and a coaxial machine gun. The Hungarian army was sufficiently impressed with the Swedish tank to obtain the licence rights in 1937 to have it built in their own country. Their locally-produced version was labelled the M38 Toldi and had a maximum armour thickness of 13mm. It weighed approximately 19,000lb.

There were a number of versions of the Toldi series placed into Hungarian army service between 1940 and 1943. The total production run was 202 vehicles. The Toldi IIa was an up-gunned version of the first model armed with a 40mm main gun and a coaxial machine gun.

Only twelve units were built of the up-armoured Toldi III, armed with a 40mm main gun and a coaxial machine gun. None were fit to deal with the Red Army's T-34 series of medium tanks or KV-1 heavy tanks and all were quickly confined to reconnaissance duties.

The only other light tank placed into service by the Hungarian army during the Second World War was designated the 40M Nimrod. A total of 135 units were built between 1942 and 1944. It was a licence-built version of a Swedish anti-aircraft tank designated the L-62 and armed with a 40mm automatic gun in a thinly-armoured open-topped turret.

The Hungarian army originally envisioned the 40M Nimrod as both a tank-killer and anti-aircraft vehicle. However, by the time it arrived on the Eastern Front it was already obsolete as a tank-killer but would prove more useful in the anti-aircraft role.

Japanese Light Tanks

In 1930, the Japanese army acquired six examples of the British Carden Lloyd VI light tank/tankette. Feeling that the British vehicle was a bit small for its requirements, the Japanese army had two up-scaled examples built with three-man crews and turret-mounted machine guns. These would include the Type 92 *Jyu-Sokosha* and the Type 94 *Tokushu Keminsha*.

Of the two new Japanese light tanks/tankettes, the approximately 7,000lb Type 94 was the more successful design with 823 units built between 1935 and 1940. Only 167 units of the approximately 8,000lb Type 92 were constructed between 1932 and 1939 as it proved unreliable in service. Maximum armour on both vehicles was 12mm thick.

The Japanese army eventually decided that machine-gun-armed light tanks/tankettes had limited battlefield usefulness. This resulted in the construction of a modified version of the Type 94 armed with a turret-mounted 37mm main gun. This vehicle was designated the Type 97 *Te-Ke*. A total of 616 units were built between 1937 and 1944. Unlike its two gasoline engine-powered predecessors, the Type 97 was powered by a diesel engine.

A New Light Tank

Another 37mm main gun-equipped Japanese light tank that began rolling off the assembly line in the late 1930s was labelled the Type 95 *Ha-Go*. Like the Type 97, it was powered by a diesel engine. As with all the Japanese light tanks, maximum armour thickness was only 12mm. A total of 2,300 units of the approximately 16,000lb vehicle were built between 1937 and 1943.

There were two attempts by the Japanese army to replace the Type 95 with a new more heavily-armoured light tank. These would include the Type 98 *Chi-Ni* and the Type 2 *Ke-To* light tanks. A total of 104 units of the Type 98 were built between 1941 and 1943. Production of the Type 2 took place between 1944 and 1945 with only thirty-four units completed before the war concluded. It is doubtful if either vehicle ever saw combat.

The Japanese navy had under its command an infantry force named the Special Naval Landing Forces (SNLF). Like the US Marine Corps, it was intended for assaulting enemy-occupied islands. For their use the Japanese navy developed an amphibious light tank armed with a 37mm main gun labelled Type 2 *Ka-Mi* (special craft). It was based on the running gear of the Type 95 with other components from the Type 2 light tank. A total of 182 were built between 1943 and 1944.

(**Opposite, above**) Taking part in a historical military vehicle event is a restored Panzer I Ausf. A. The elderly gentleman in the turret of the vehicle served on the Panzer I series in his youth and had assisted in restoring the tank to running condition. The vehicle's paint scheme and markings match those from the German military invasion of Poland in 1939. (*Thomas Anderson*)

(**Opposite, below**) Pictured on display is an unrestored Panzer I Ausf. A. The large horizontal steel girder along the suspension system acted as a reinforcing beam for the last four road wheels on either side of the vehicle's hull. The rearmost road wheels on either side of the hull acted as idlers, which kept the tracks tensioned. (*Author's collection*)

(**Above**) Arriving in North Africa in February 1942 is a Panzer I Ausf. A. Power for the tank was provided by an air-cooled Krupp gasoline engine. On very early production units of the tank the engine tended to overheat due to insufficient ventilation. This was solved by the addition of the large air scoop seen on the roof of the rear engine deck of the vehicle pictured. (*National Archives*)

(**Opposite, above**) Taking part in the German invasion of Norway that began in April 1940 is this Panzer I Ausf. A. The vehicle's manually-operated turret was armed with two machine guns. The tank had a length of 13ft 2in, a width of 6ft 9in and a height of 5ft 8in. (*Patton Museum*)

(**Opposite, below**) No doubt assembled for a pre-war parade is this formation of Panzer I Ausf. A light tanks. The tank's turret is offset to the right-hand side of the upper hull to allow room for the driver's hatch on the left-hand side of the upper hull. The vehicle commander, who also acted as the gunner, sat on a seat suspended from the underside of the turret roof. (*Patton Museum*)

The front road wheels on either side of the Panzer I Ausf. A hull were independently sprung on coil springs, one of which is visible in this photograph. Large hydraulic shock absorbers were connected in parallel with the springs. The remaining road wheels on the tank were set in articulated pairs that mounted on a single arm pivoted at the centre, which connected to leaf springs. (*Patton Museum*)

Because the original engine in the Panzer I Ausf. A proved underpowered, a second version of the tank shown in this pre-war photograph was fitted with a new more powerful engine and designated the Panzer I Ausf. B. To accommodate the new larger engine the rear hull of the Panzer I Ausf. B was redesigned, which resulted in the lengthening of the tank to 14ft 6in. (*Patton Museum*)

Shown here on display at a US army museum is this Panzer I Ausf. B. The upper rear deck on this particular vehicle is not the original and is a poorly-done post-war reproduction. The lengthening of the hull on the Panzer I Ausf. B required an extra road wheel on either side of the tank as well as a dedicated raised idler. Both these design features are visible in this photograph. (*Christophe Vallier*)

In this picture we see an unrestored Panzer I Ausf. B on display as a monument vehicle at a Spanish army base. The vehicle commander on both models of the Panzer I aimed the turret-mounted machine guns with a 2.5 power telescopic sight located in-between the two weapons. There was authorized storage on the tank for 2,250 rounds of 7.92mm ammunition. (*Patton Museum*)

(**Opposite, above**) Pictured is a dedicated reconnaissance vehicle based on the Panzer I series and designated the Panzer I Ausf. C. Besides having thicker armour than the previous two models of the Panzer I series, it was also much faster as it rode on a suspension system consisting of large interleaved road wheels connected by torsion bars. Main armament was the EW 141 anti-tank rifle of which less than 100 were built. (*Patton Museum*)

(**Above**) On display at an Eastern European museum is a Panzer I Ausf. F, which was a heavily-armoured version of the Panzer I intended for the infantry support role. Its armour would have protected it from many of the anti-tank weapons in the early war period. However, the fact that its main armament was two machine guns meant that it would have been unable to deal with enemy defensive fortifications. (*Patton Museum*)

(**Opposite, below**) Before production of the Panzer II series began, 100 pre-production units were built to see which design features worked and which did not. They were divided between four different models. The vehicle pictured is one of the pilots and was assigned the designation Panzer I Ausf. B. Note the vehicle commander's two-piece split hatch. (*Patton Museum*)

(**Above**) An early-production model of the Panzer II is shown riding on the standard suspension system for the series. It consisted of front hull-mounted drive sprockets and rear hull idlers with large road wheels connected to quarter-elliptical leaf springs. As with the experimental Panzer II units, the vehicle pictured has the original vehicle commander's two-piece split hatch. (*Patton Museum*)

(**Opposite, above**) Pictured is a preserved Panzer II from one of the first four production models. It can be identified as such by the upper front vertical hull armour plate constructed of two pieces with the right-hand side plate angled rearwards. The German army eventually had 20mm thick steel armour plates bolted to the two upper front vertical hull plates as is visible on the vehicle shown here. (*Christophe Vallier*)

(**Opposite, below**) The final production model of the Panzer II series built in relatively large numbers was labelled the Ausf. F. Pictured is a restored example. Unlike the two-piece upper front vertical hull plates on earlier models of the tank, the Panzer Ausf. F version has a straight one-piece vertical hull plate visible in this photograph. (*Tank Museum*)

Pictured here is a restored and running example of a Panzer II Ausf. F. It is 15ft 9in in length with a width of 7ft 6in and a height of 7ft. Due to complaints about the poor level of protection offered by the original vehicle commander's two-piece split hatch, a new vehicle commander's cupola with eight periscopes was developed and is seen on the Panzer II Ausf. F shown here. The turret of the tank was offset to the left centreline of the vehicle and manned by the vehicle commander/gunner. He sat on a seat suspended from the turret roof. The driver was seated in the front hull and the radioman under the turret in a rearward-facing seat. (*Thomas Anderson*)

In this close-up photograph of a Panzer II Ausf. F we can see the dummy armour visor made out of aluminium on the left-hand side of the single-piece front vertical hull plate. It was intended to confuse anti-tank gunners taking aim at the tank. The single-piece front vertical hull plate on the Ausf. F was 30mm thick. (*Patton Museum*)

The 20mm main gun mounted on the preserved Panzer II Ausf. F pictured here was based on a ground-based anti-aircraft gun and as such could only be fired in full automatic. The weapon was fed from ten-round magazines. There was authorized storage for 180 rounds of 20mm ammunition on board the Panzer II series, divided between armour-piercing (AP) and high-explosive (HE). (*Christophe Vallier*)

(**Opposite, above**) German industry was tasked in 1939 with the development of a dedicated reconnaissance model of the Panzer II series. That vehicle would eventually be designated the Panzer II Ausf. L and named the *Luchs* (Lynx). Pictured is a preserved example. The first prototype of the vehicle appeared in 1942 with production beginning the following year. (*Christophe Vallier*)

(**Opposite, below**) Unlike the earlier production versions of the Panzer II series that had been fitted with armoured vision ports on all four sides of their turrets, the Panzer II Ausf. L *Luchs* turret had no armoured vision ports. Instead, they had two turret roof-mounted rotating periscopes. The vehicle had a crew of four: vehicle commander, gunner, radio-operator and driver. (*Tank Museum*)

(**Above**) Shown here in pre-war Czech army service is an LT vz.35. It had entered into front-line service with the Czech army in 1936. When taken into German army service in 1939 the LT vz.35 was designated the Panzer 35(t). In this picture we can see the forward-firing 7.92mm machine gun fitted in its own separate ball mount in the turret and another in the front hull. (*Tank Museum*)

Pictured is a restored Czech-designed and built light tank labelled the LT vz.35. It is painted in a pre-war Czech army three-tone camouflage scheme. The painted cowling extending on top of the tank's 37mm main gun is an armoured housing for the weapon's recoil cylinder. Missing from the vehicle pictured is the turret-mounted forward-firing 7.92mm machine gun. (*Christophe Vallier*)

Unlike its German-designed and built counterparts, the Czech-designed and built LT vz.35 had its transmission and drive sprockets located in the rear of the hull. Instead of the welded construction of the German army light tanks the LT vz.35 was of riveted and bolted construction as is evident in this photograph. (*Patton Museum*)

On display at an Eastern European military museum is this unrestored LT vz.35 missing its armament. Besides serving with the German army up through to 1942 as a gun tank it also served with some of Germany's wartime allies' armies. The tank itself is 16ft in length, had a width of 6ft 10in and a height of 7ft 8in. (*Thomas Anderson*)

(**Opposite, above**) Pre-war Czech army unhappiness with the poor reliability of the LT vz.35 led to Czech industry designing and building an improved light tank labelled the LT vz.38. When taken into German army service the tank was designated the Panzer 38(t). In this photograph we see a preserved example of a Panzer 38(t) in a German army early-war paint scheme and markings. (*Bob Fleming*)

(**Opposite, below**) The Czech-built Panzer 38(t) featured the same crew and armament arrangement as the earlier Panzer 35(t), which included a 37mm main gun and two machine guns. Unlike the Panzer 35(t) that had a rear hull-mounted transmission and drive sprockets, the Panzer 38(t) had a front hull-mounted transmission and drive sprockets. (*Charles Kliment collection*)

(**Above**) A wartime photograph of a German army Panzer 38(t). The lack of a front hull-mounted 7.92mm machine gun on this particular vehicle identifies it as a company or battalion commander vehicle. Regimental or divisional commanders' versions of the Panzer 38(t) also lacked the bow machine gun and had the 37mm main gun replaced with a wooden mock-up. (*National Archives*)

(**Opposite, above**) In a German museum we see a restored Panzer 38(t). It, like the earlier Panzer 35(t), was powered by liquid-cooled gasoline engines. The vehicle commander's cupola has four episcopes and a rotating peri-scope in its own armoured mount as is visible on the vehicle pictured. The Panzer 38(t) has a length of 15ft 1in, a width of 6ft 11in and a height of 7ft 10in. (*Frank Schulz*)

(**Opposite, below**) As with the Panzer I and Panzer II the German army explored the development of a dedicated reconnaissance version of the Panzer 38(t). The resulting four-man prototype vehicle pictured was labelled the Panzer 38(t) neuer Art. Only five were constructed, with three being of welded construction as is the vehicle shown and the other two of riveted construction. (*Charles Kliment collection*)

(**Above**) As a general rule the majority of captured tanks employed by the German army during the Second World War performed in the internal security role. One example of that would be the Polish army 7TP light tank seen here in a pre-war parade. Armed with a 37mm main gun and a single machine gun, the vehicle was designated the Panzer 7TP(p) by the German army. (*Tank Museum*)

(**Above**) In the summer of 1940, the German army acquired a large inventory of former French army tanks. The oldest among them was the First World War vintage FT light tanks. Pictured is a preserved example. In German army service the two-man tank when armed with a 37mm main gun was labelled the Panzer 730c(f) and when armed only with a machine gun the Panzer 730m(f). (*Pierre Olivier*)

(**Opposite, above**) Pictured is a column of machine-gun-armed Panzer 730m(f) light tanks. The small dome on the roof of the vehicle's turrets was for ventilation. The ingress and egress point for the vehicle commander was by way of a small downward-folding hatch at the rear of the turret. As is visible in this picture it was also employed by the vehicle commanders to sit on when not engaged in combat. (*Patton Museum*)

(**Opposite, below**) The most modern former French army light tanks placed into service by the German army were the very similar-looking Renault R-35 and Hotchkiss H-35. This particular vehicle pictured is easily identified as a Hotchkiss H-35 by the builder's name cast into the lower front hull armour. In German army service it was designated the Panzer 35H 734(f). (*Patton Museum*)

(**Opposite, above**) Pictured is a preserved French-built Hotchkiss H-39 light tank in an Israeli museum. It featured a longer-barrelled, higher-velocity 37mm main gun than its predecessor the Hotchkiss H-35. In German army service it was designated the Panzer 38H 735(f). The vehicle is 13ft 10in in length, has a width of 6ft 1in and a height of 6ft 7in. (*Vladimir Yakubov*)

(**Opposite, below**) As Italy was on the side of the allies in the First World War it was provided with a single example of the French-designed and built FT light tank in 1918. An Italian production version seen here appeared in 1923. It was both lighter and faster than the French version and was designated the Fiat 3000 and would remain in Italian army service until 1943. (*Patton Museum*)

(**Above**) The Italian army purchased a small number of two-man turretless British machine-gun-armed light tanks in the late 1920s. The Italian-built copies were labelled the *Carro Veloce* 29. Continued modifications to the tank's design by Italian industry led to the production of a vehicle labelled the *Carro Veloce* 33 or CV-33, which is seen here on a pre-war training activity. (*Tank Museum*)

(**Opposite, above**) The two-man Italian army CV-33 had a length of 10ft 5in, a width of 4ft 7in and a height of only 3ft 11in. The crew of the CV-33 seen here and the follow-on models consisted of the vehicle commander/gunner and the driver. The vehicle could be armed with either one or two forward-firing machine guns. Ingress and egress from the vehicles was provided by two overhead hatches. (*Tank Museum*)

(**Above**) Somewhere in North Africa a Commonwealth armoured car is shown towing a captured Italian army CV-33, for what purpose could be an interesting story in itself. Power for the CV-33 series came from liquid-cooled gasoline engines, which had to be hand-cranked to start. Maximum operational range of the vehicle series was approximately 80 miles. (*Tank Museum*)

(**Opposite, below**) Awareness of the fact that machine-gun-armed light tanks had limited effectiveness on the modern battlefield pushed the Italian army to ask for an up-armed light tank in the second half of the 1930s. Italian industry eventually came up with the two-man L6/40 light tank seen here in 1939 armed with a 20mm main gun. (*Tank Museum*)

(**Opposite, above**) In 1936, the Hungarian army acquired a single example of the Swedish Landsverk L60 light tank for test purposes. Positive results led to a modified licence-built version being built for the Hungarian army, designated the 38M *Toldi* or *Toldi* I, with an up-armoured version labelled the *Toldi* II. Pictured is a preserved Swedish army version of the Landsverk L60 light tank designated the M/40L. (*Tank Museum*)

(**Above**) A unit of Hungarian army *Toldi* I or *Toldi* II light tanks is shown taking part in a parade. Instead of the 37mm main gun of the Swedish Landsverk L60 light tank, the *Toldi* I and II were armed with a 20mm main gun. The three-man tank has a length of 15ft 7in, a width of 7ft and a height of 6ft 2in. (*Charles Kliment collection*)

(**Opposite, below**) The 20mm main gun on the Hungarian army *Toldi* I and *Toldi* II light tanks proved completely inadequate on the Eastern Front. This resulted in up-gunning the vehicle with a 40mm main gun as seen here and the designation *Toldi* IIa. An up-armoured version of the *Toldi* IIa was referred to as the *Toldi* III. (*Charles Kliment collection*)

(**Opposite, above**) Upon the lengthened chassis of their Landsverk L60 light tank the Swedish army took into service an anti-aircraft version designated the L-62. It was armed with a single 40mm main gun in an open-topped turret. A licence-built Hungarian army version seen here based on the chassis of the *Toldi* I was referred to as the 'Nimrod'. (*Charles Kliment collection*)

(**Above**) Prior to the Second World War Czechoslovak industry marketed a number of their light tank designs to foreign armies, including the machine-gun-armed AH-IV seen here. The Romanian army took into service a slightly different version labelled by the builder originally as the AH-IV-R and later as the R-1. Armour protection on the vehicle was a maximum of 12mm. (*Charles Kliment collection*)

(**Opposite, below**) Pictured is the three-man Japanese army Type 92 *Jyu-Sokosha* light tank. Field use quickly demonstrated that the Type 92 was both under-armed and under-armoured with a maximum armour thickness of only 6mm. Another issue concerned the vehicle's suspension system that had to be redesigned several times during its production run to provide an adequate level of off-road performance. (*Tank Museum*)

The Japanese army's replacement for the failed Type 92 light tank was the Type 94 TK (special tractor) light tank seen here in this retouched photograph. Armed with only a single machine gun, the two-man vehicle was also fitted with a trailer hitch so that it could tow tracked supply trailers. The Type 94 was 9ft 10in in length with a width of 5ft 3in and a height of 5ft 3in. (*Tank Museum*)

(**Opposite, above**) An American Marine is examining a knocked-out Japanese army Type 94 TK light tank. It was the most numerous Japanese army light tank in the 1930s because it was affordable. The Type 94 was adequate when confronting enemy infantry units lacking tanks of their own or dedicated anti-tank weapons. Against better-armed opponents it was not viable on the battlefield. (*National Archives*)

(**Opposite, below**) The two-man Japanese army Type 97 *Tokushu Keninsha* (Special Tractor) light tank was also referred to as the *Te-Ke* light tank. It had a length of 12ft 1in, a width of 5ft 11in and a height of 5ft 10in. Unlike the Type 92 light tank powered by an air-cooled gasoline engine, the Type 97 received power from an air-cooled diesel engine. (*Tank Museum*)

(**Opposite, above**) US Marines are looking over a captured Japanese army Type 97 *Tokushu Keninsha* (Special Tractor) light tank. It is armed with a turret-mounted 37mm main gun not visible in this picture. There was authorized storage for ninety-six main gun rounds in the vehicle. The tank was of riveted construction with a maximum armour thickness of 12mm. (*National Archives*)

(**Opposite, below**) Pictured on display at the now-closed US army Ordnance Museum is this unrestored Japanese army Type 95 *Ha-Go* light tank. Power for the vehicle came from an air-cooled diesel engine that provided it with a maximum operational range of approximately 155 miles. The drive sprockets and transmission were in the front hull. (*Author's collection*)

(**Above**) A Japanese soldier is shown guiding a Type 95 *Ha-Go* light tank to a collection area at the end of the Second World War. The vehicle was armed with the same 37mm main gun that went into the Type 97 light tank. Besides the main gun the Type 95 was armed with two machine guns, which are visible in this photograph: one in the front hull and the other in the rear of the turret. (*Patton Museum*)

Shown here on display at a British museum is a Type 95 *Ha-Go* light tank. It is painted in a camouflage scheme similar to what the vehicle might have sported during the Second World War. The 37mm main gun on the tank fired an armour-piercing (AP) round that could penetrate a vertical armour plate 40mm thick at a range of 546 yards. There was authorized storage for 130 main gun rounds in the vehicle. (*Tank Museum*)

In this comparison photograph we see a restored Type 95 *Ha-Go* light tank parked alongside a restored American M4 series medium tank armed with a 75mm main gun. The Type 95 weighs approximately 16,000lb, is 14ft 4in in length with a width of 6ft 9in and a height of 7ft 2in. (*Author's collection*)

In this poor-quality image we see the Japanese army Type 98 *Chi-Ni* light tank. It was a redesigned and upgraded version of the Type 95 *Ha-Go* light tank. The main gun was still 37mm but offered a higher muzzle velocity and hence greater armour penetration. Because the armour was thicker on the Type 98, it required a more powerful air-cooled diesel engine. (*Tank Museum*)

An amphibious light tank placed into service by the Japanese navy during the Second World War is seen here after being captured. It was labelled the Type 2 *Ka-Mi* (Special Craft) and rode on a Type 95 *Ha-Go* light tank suspension system. The 37mm gun-armed turret came from the Type 2 *Ke-To* light tank of which only a small number were built. (*Patton Museum*)

Allied troops are shown posing upon a number of captured Japanese navy Type 2 *Ka-Mi* amphibious light tanks. These particular vehicles are missing the large forward and rear pontoons that provided them with the buoyancy they needed in the water to float. Upon landing the pontoons could be released and the vehicle could therefore function as a normal gun tank. (*Patton Museum*)

Chapter Two

Early-War Medium Tanks

In January 1934, the German army held an important conference. It was at this time they decided that for the near future not one but two medium tanks would be required for equipping the new Panzer divisions. Each new five-man medium tank would undertake a different battlefield role. The concept of a multi-purpose tank did not yet exist in German army thinking at the time, neither did it exist in any other tank-equipped army of the day.

Panzer III

The smaller and lighter of the two medium tanks ordered by the German army was designated the Panzer III. The first examples of the tank began rolling off the assembly lines in 1936. By the time production ceased in late 1943 a total of 5,774 units had been constructed. Daimler-Benz designed the Panzer III but was joined in its production by a number of other manufacturers as was typical for all mass-produced German-designed and built tanks.

The German army considered the Panzer III a *Sturmwagen* (assault tank) with its main weapon being its three machine guns. In case it might encounter enemy tanks, the Panzer III was armed with a small-calibre, high-velocity main gun, optimized for firing armour-piercing (AP) rounds. Combat experience during the invasion of France quickly demonstrated to the German army that the high-velocity gun on the Panzer III was its main armament and not its machine guns.

The initial version of the Panzer III weighed approximately 34,000lb with the final model rising to a weight of around 52,000lb. This occurred due to additional armour and larger main guns being fitted to the tank. The Panzer III's original ordnance inventory number was 141. Late-production Panzer IIIs, depending on the weapon fitted, could be assigned the ordnance inventory number 141/1, 141/2 or 141/3.

Panzer III Firepower

The first production model of the Panzer III was armed with a 37mm high-velocity main gun designated the 3.7cm KwK L/45 and machine guns. It had a barrel length of 5ft 6in. Firing its standard all-steel armour-piercing round at 2,440 ft/sec, it could penetrate 22mm of armour at a range of 1,094 yards. It was selected for the Panzer III because of its commonality of ammunition with the towed anti-tank version designated the 3.7cm PaK 36, which entered service in 1934 with the German army infantry branch.

In the US army and the British army all-steel AP rounds are referred to as 'shot'. All AP tank rounds in German are referred to as *Panzergranate* or PzGr. and were assigned identification numbers in wartime documents.

The 37mm main gun on the early versions of the Panzer III series was not the preferred weapon of choice among many. They believed that it should have been armed with a 50mm main gun. Combat experience during the German invasion of France proved the naysayers correct. Later versions of the Panzer III were up-armed with a 50mm main gun designated the 5cm KwK 38 L/42. It had a barrel length of 6ft 9in.

The British army identified the up-gunning of the Panzer III during the fighting in North Africa as is seen in this passage from a report dated October 1941: 'The mounting of the 50mm QF [quick-firing] gun in the Pz.Kpfw.III is the only innovation encountered in the armament. This has been expected for some time by the British General Staff, as the original 37mm gun has not proved sufficiently effective against British AFVs in France.'

Different AP Rounds

Besides the 50mm AP shot round there was an APC (armour-piercing capped) round. It consisted of a strong blunt-nosed steel penetrative cap fitted over the blunt nose of a standard AP shot projectile. The penetrative cap reduced the odds of the projectile shattering upon contact with face-hardened armour plate and turned the projectile into sloping armour rather than being deflected off it.

As the 50mm APC rounds fired by the Panzer III contained a high-explosive (HE) filler, they could also be designated APC-HE or AP-HE rounds. The effectiveness of this combination is attested to in a British army report dated May 1942:

> The German projectiles which caused the greatest amount of damage to Allied tanks in the Western Desert Campaign have been the AP-HE type ... These projectiles at long ranges need only to obtain a partial penetration and the explosive charge can complete the destruction of at least the tank crew. At closer ranges the destructive effect is very great, where in many cases destruction of the tank is permanent.

To reduce air resistance most wartime APC-HE rounds were eventually fitted with sharply-pointed, lightweight nose fairings. By reducing air resistance the muzzle velocity was increased, which in turn improved range and armour penetration capabilities. In British army nomenclature APC-HE rounds fitted with a nose fairing became an APCBC (armour-piercing capped, ballistic cap) round or APCBC-HE round. The US army retained the APC-HE classification for the round when fitted with a nose fairing.

Sub-Calibre AP Round

There was also another type of AP round for the 50mm main gun on the Panzer III. It consisted of a tungsten sub-calibre core projectile centred in a lightweight metal carrier. When the round was fired the carrier travelled to the target along with the sub-calibre core projectile. The German designation for this type of round was PzGr. 40 regardless of the calibre of the round. It was always in short supply due to the need for tungsten by German industry for its machine tools.

The effectiveness of the PzGr. 40 rounds dropped off at longer ranges due to gravity and wind resistance upon the carrier. This in turn lowered the muzzle velocity of the sub-calibre core projectiles and hence their range and penetration capabilities. The US army classified the PzGr. 40 rounds as HVAP (hyper-velocity, armour-piercing) rounds. In the British army it was classified as APCR (armour-piercing, composite rigid) rounds, a designation the author will continue throughout this work.

In the 1950s, an updated APCR round was developed for tank guns. It was labelled an APDS (armour-piercing discarding sabot) round. It differed from its Second World War predecessor because only the sub-calibre core travels to the target. The carrier, known as the 'sabot', is peeled off the core by wind resistance as soon as it exits a tank barrel.

Another 50mm Tank Gun

The problem with arming the Panzer III with the 5cm KwK 38 L/42 main gun was the fact that Hitler had demanded that it be armed with a longer-barrelled 50mm main gun. That gun was designated the 5cm KwK 39 L/60 and had a barrel length of 9ft 9in. Hitler's order had been ignored for two reasons: firstly, there was a shortage of the weapon and secondly, the German army believed that the shorter 50mm main gun could deal with any future battlefield threats.

The standard APCBC-HE round for the short-barrelled 50mm main gun had a muzzle velocity of 2,740 ft/sec and could penetrate 48mm of armour at a range of 1,094 yards. The gun's PzGr. 40 round had a muzzle velocity of 3,871 ft/sec. It could penetrate 38mm of armour at 1,094 yards. However, at a range of 546 yards the PzGr. 40 round could penetrate 72mm of armour in comparison to the standard APCBC-HE round that could only penetrate 59mm of armour.

The first 50mm main gun-armed Panzer IIIs arrived in North Africa in January 1942. From a captured German army report is this passage recording the effectiveness of the 50mm main gun APCBC-HE rounds carried on board the Panzer III:

> Mark II [Matilda] is the British infantry tank which has a speed of about 25km (15 miles) per hour. The armour on the front is 80mm (3.15 inches) backed by

concrete, and it carries a 40mm (1.6 inch) gun. The British generally use these tanks in a close formation of a front of fire … An equal number of Panzer *Kampfwagen* III [tanks] should thrust at full speed, without stopping to fire, at the flank of the enemy tanks until they are within a range of 300 metres (330 yards), and then open fire, using alternately AP-HE (armour-piercing high-explosive) shells and AP (armour-piercing) nose-fuze shells. [British] Infantry tanks are easily set on fire [with] 50mm (2 inch) shell [which] pierces clean at 300 metres (330 yards).

The End of the Line

The invasion of the Soviet Union had quickly demonstrated that the short-barrelled 50mm main gun on the Panzer III was inadequate when dealing with the Red Army T-34 medium tank or KV-1 heavy tank. Upon learning that his orders to up-arm the Panzer III series had been ignored, Hitler was incensed. This quickly resulted in all new production models of the Panzer III coming off the assembly line, starting in December 1941, with a longer-barrelled 50mm main gun.

Many of the earlier versions of the Panzer III were eventually retrofitted with the longer 50mm main gun as per Hitler's order. Despite up-arming the Panzer III, the tank was obsolete on the battlefields of the Eastern Front by the summer of 1942.

Authorized main gun ammunition storage capacity varied between the different versions of the Panzer III. The Panzer III series tanks armed with the 37mm main gun carried anywhere between 121 and 150 main gun rounds. With the up-arming of the Panzer III series tank with the two different types of 50mm main guns, ammunition capacity ranged between eighty-four and ninety-nine main gun rounds depending on the model of tank.

Panzer III Armour Protection

Like its main armament, the armour protection levels of the Panzer III series were constantly upgraded during its time in service. The first four models of the Panzer III, the Ausf. A through to the Ausf. D, had a maximum armour protection thickness of only 15mm. This thin armour reflected the German army's pre-war emphasis on mobility over firepower and protection. An excellent example of that preoccupation with tank mobility was put forward by German army General Heinz Guderian in 1936:

> The attack by tanks must be conducted with maximum acceleration in order to exploit the advantage of surprise, to penetrate deep into enemy lines, to prevent reserves from intervening, and to extend the tactical success into a strategical victory. Speed, therefore, is what is to be exacted above anything else from the armoured weapon [tanks]. Speed makes possible the maximum degree of surprise because it overcomes delay in concentrating forces at chosen points. Speed neutralizes the enemy defence by limiting the possibilities of fire from his anti-tank weapons.

The Panzer III Ausf. B through to Ausf. D saw combat in Poland in September 1939 and their armour protection levels and suspension systems were considered unsatisfactory. None would remain in service for the invasion of France and the Low Countries. Subsequent versions of the Panzer III would be up-armoured at the factory with add-on armour kits, despite the reduction in their speed and range.

The British army had noticed during the fighting in North Africa the use of add-on armour kits by the German army for its medium tanks. This up-armouring of not just the Panzer III but Panzer IV is mentioned in a British report dated October 1941:

> The thickness of armour on the German tanks will be seen to be in excess of what was originally thought … Instead of redesigning their tanks straight away when they discovered that the armour protection was inadequate, the Germans have overcome their difficulties by welding or bolting supplementary plates of armour on those places, which by experience they have discovered are the most vulnerable spots. In this way their tank production has not been interfered with.

The Panzer III Ausf. E, which was the first model ordered into large-scale production, had a maximum base armour thickness of 30mm. This thicker and heavier armour on the Ausf. E was possible because of a new more robust torsion bar suspension system, which featured on all subsequent Panzer III series tanks.

Beginning with the Panzer III Ausf. G, the maximum base armour thickness went to 37mm and was then raised to 50mm on the Panzer III Ausf. J and follow-on models. This does not count any additional add-on armour kits added to various versions of the Panzer III from the Ausf. E through to the final Ausf. N model.

One of the best-known add-on armour kits for the later models of the Panzer III was the fitting of thin-spaced armour plates around the turret and hull/superstructure of the tanks. In the German language they were referred to as *Schuerzen*, which translates as protective skirts.

Final Model of the Panzer III

The last model of the Panzer III, labelled the Ausf. N, was armed with a low-velocity 75mm gun. It then became an escort (fire-support) tank for the Tiger E heavy tank. Anticipated targets included anti-tank guns, defensive positions and infantry. Production of the Panzer III Ausf. N began in June 1942 and continued through to August 1943. It had authorized storage for sixty-four main gun rounds.

The British army first noticed the Panzer III Ausf. N in North Africa, as documented in this extract from a British army Technical Intelligence Summary dated January 1943:

> Another recent development is the appearance of Pz.Kpfw.IIIs mounted with what appears to be the old short 7.5cm KwK. These tanks have hull side loading doors and apart from the gun barrel appears to be identical with Model L ... During an assault, the Pz.Kpfw.VIs [Tiger Es] would attack hostile heavy tank battalions or heavy pillboxes, and the Pz.Kpfw.IIIs would attack machine-gun nests or lighter tanks.

Panzer IV

The larger and heavier of the two medium tanks ordered into production by the German army in 1937 was labelled the Panzer IV and designed by Krupp. The vehicle's ordnance inventory number was 161. It was originally armed with a low-velocity, short-barrelled 75mm main gun optimized for firing HE rounds at non-armoured or thinly-armoured targets. It was also armed with machine guns.

The German army classified the Panzer IV as an escort (fire-support) tank for the smaller and lighter Panzer I through Panzer III tanks. The initial production version weighed approximately 41,000lb. In its last configuration the tank weighed about 56,000lb. Late-production Panzer IVs, depending on the weapon fitted, could be assigned the ordnance inventory number 161/1 or 161/2.

In March 1942, the Panzer IV was armed with a new high-velocity long-barrelled 75mm main gun capable of destroying all the Allied tanks then in service. With the new gun the Panzer IV became an all-purpose tank capable of engaging armoured and non-armoured targets with either AP or HE rounds. Production of the Panzer IV series was undertaken by a number of different firms and continued till the end of the war in Europe with 8,569 units built.

Low-Velocity 75mm Main Gun

The low-velocity, short-barrelled 75mm main gun on the early production Panzer IV tanks was 5ft 9in in length and designated the 7.5cm KwK 37 L/24. The weapon was nicknamed the 'cigar butt' by the crews of the Panzer IV.

The intended role for the 7.5cm KwK 37 L/24 was to fire HE rounds at non-armoured or thinly-armoured targets. In German, HE tank rounds are referred to as *Sprenggranate* or just *SprGr* in wartime documents and assigned identification numbers. When confronted with an enemy tank the crew could employ an APC-HE round with a muzzle velocity of 1,260 ft/sec. It could penetrate 35mm of armour at a range of 1,094 yards.

There was also a *Granate Hohlladung* (hollow-charge shell), which had an official designation as the 7.5cm Pz.Gr.Patr. KwK 38. It came in four progressively-improved versions labelled the GR 38H1 through to GR 38H1/C. Other names for this type of round now include 'shaped charge' or HEAT (high-explosive anti-tank).

The German army had considered at one point arming the Panzer IV with a long-barrelled, high-velocity 75mm main gun before it went into production. This was due to information that indicated a new generation of French tanks boasting armour up to 40mm thick. However, in the end it was decided to stay with the short-barrelled, low-velocity 75mm gun and its existing APC and hollow-charge rounds.

Combat action in France showed that the APC-HE and the hollow-charge rounds fired by the 7.5cm KwK 37 L/24 gun on the Panzer IV were useless against some thickly-armoured French and British tanks. Despite this evidence, the effort to up-arm the Panzer IV with a long-barrelled, high-velocity 75mm gun languished until the invasion of the Soviet Union, when the German army was confronted with the fact that once again the tank-killing rounds fired by the 7.5cm KwK 37 L/24 gun lacked the ability to destroy well-armoured enemy medium and heavy tanks.

High-Velocity 75mm Guns

To address the design shortcomings of the 7.5cm KwK 37 L/24 gun mounted on the early-production Panzer IV, a new long-barrelled, high-velocity 75mm gun designated the 7.5cm KwK 40 L/43 appeared. It had a barrel length of 10ft 6in. As with the previous 75mm gun, the new 75mm gun was provided with hollow-charge rounds. The standard APCBC round it fired had a muzzle velocity of 2,426 ft/sec and could penetrate 81mm of armour at a range of 1,094 yards.

In early 1943, German industry began installing on new-production Panzer IVs an even more powerful 75mm tank gun designated the 7.5cm KwK 40 L/48. Its barrel was 11ft 8in long. The added length of the barrel pushed up the gun's standard APCBC-HE round to a muzzle velocity of 2,591 ft/sec. This meant it could penetrate 85mm of armour at a range of 1,094 yards. There was also a Pz.Gr. 40 round for the 7.5cm KwK 40 L/48 on the late-production Panzer IVs. No hollow-charge rounds were provided for the weapon due to their limited battlefield effectiveness.

Besides the different types of AP rounds, all the 75mm main guns on the Panzer IV series were provided with a smoke round. Its employment is described in an August 1944 US army publication titled the *Intelligence Bulletin*:

As a rule German tanks employ smoke shells to achieve surprise, to conceal a change of direction, and to cover a withdrawal. The shells normally are fired to land almost 100 yards in front of an Allied Force. There are no reports to indicate that smoke shells are used in range estimation.

Authorized main gun storage for the Panzer IV series ranged between eighty-four and ninety-nine rounds depending on the model of the tank. However, it was not uncommon for the tank crews of all the combatants of the Second World War to load more main gun rounds into their vehicles than they were authorized to carry.

Protection

The first production model of the Panzer IV had the same 15mm thick base armour protection as the Panzer III, which was intended to be proof against machine-gun fire only. As with the former, the Panzer IV was continuously up-armoured throughout its service life. The maximum base armour thickness on the last version of the Panzer IV was 80mm.

As with the Panzer III, the Panzer IV was often fitted with add-on armour kits applied at the factory and some improvised armour kits in the field, including *Schuerzen*. The downside of this constant up-armouring of the Panzer III and Panzer IV was the fact that the vehicles were never intended to carry as much weight as they did. That thought is seen in this passage from a German POW in a 1944 British army report:

> [The] P/W refers to loss of manoeuvrability and speed of the Pz.Kpfw.III and IV owing to the increased weight, mainly due to thicker armour and bigger guns. He says that Pz.Kpfw.III had stood up well but that the Pz.Kpfw.IV had become nose-heavy as a result of the fitting of the 7.5cm long gun, to such an extent that the front springs [are] always bent and the tank sways about.

Tank Layout and Crew Positions

The Panzer III and Panzer IV had the same basic design layout with the vehicles divided from front to back into three separate compartments. At the front of each tank hull was the driver's compartment, with the driver on the left side and the radio-operator. Their positions were separated by the vehicle's front hull-mounted transmissions.

Due to the fact that the Panzer III was smaller than the Panzer IV, the driver and radio-operator lacked the overhead hatches provided on the Panzer IV. Their normal ingress or egress path was through side turret hatches on the Ausf. A through to Ausf. D models. Beginning with the Panzer III Ausf. E, which began production in 1938, side hull hatches were also provided.

The fighting compartment of both tanks was located in the centre of the vehicles' hulls and surmounted by their three-man turrets, which housed the tank commander, gunner and loader. On the right of the main gun breech was the loader and on the left-hand side, directly in front of and below the tank commander, the gunner's position. This was the opposite arrangement to the American M4 series of medium tanks.

The tank commander's position on a Panzer III, which was the same on a Panzer IV, is described in a Western Allied informational booklet released in October 1944: 'The commander sits in the middle at the rear of the turret, directly behind the main armament. His cupola is integral with the turret, and six ports fitted with bulletproof glass blocks and sliding steel shutters provide all-around vision. The cupola hatch consists of two hinged flaps.'

In the rear compartment of the Panzer III and Panzer IV were liquid-cooled twelve-cylinder Maybach gasoline-powered engines of varying horsepower ratings. They were separated from the fighting compartment by a bulkhead. Located to the rear of the engines were the radiators.

Working Together in Combat

From a July 1942 US army publication is this extract describing how the German army Panzer III and Panzer IV (armed with the short-barrelled low-velocity 75mm main gun) worked in conjunction on the battlefields of North Africa:

> He first engages our anti-tank guns and artillery with his Mark IV tanks and supporting guns; meanwhile, Mark III tanks form up for the assault and frequently challenge the defended area at different points in strong compact formations. Then, having decided where to launch his main thrust and having endeavoured to reduce the power of the defence by the fire of his Mark IV tanks and artillery, he launches a strong attack with his Mark III tanks followed by motorized infantry and guns direct on his objective ... As a rule, the Germans try to develop a pincer movement, the two lines of advance converging on the final objective. An attacking column will move fast and straight to its objective irrespective of events elsewhere.

Captured Medium Tanks

Besides employing captured French army light tanks in the training and internal security roles during the Second World War, the German army did the same with the French army medium tanks it acquired. The Somua S-35 became the Panzer 35-S 739(f) and the Chat B-1 bis the Panzer B-2 740(f). As with their light tank counterparts, some of the captured French army medium tanks would see service in German-occupied countries and all but disappear from German army service by 1944.

The battlefield successes of the German army on the Eastern Front between 1941 into the early part of 1943 led to the acquisition of a relatively large number of T-34 medium tanks, armed with the 76.2mm main gun, in various versions. The majority would eventually be sent to the smelters in Germany with a much smaller number being retained by German army units on the Eastern Front. Some were eventually transferred to Germany's wartime allies.

Those former Red Army T-34 medium tanks pressed into German army service on the Eastern Front were referred to as the Panzer T-34 747(r). Some were fitted with German radios and a few with the tank commander cupolas from knocked-out Panzer III and Panzer IV medium tanks.

As with any captured tanks pressed into front-line service by the German army against its former owners, the captured Red Army T-34 medium tanks had been painted with large over-sized German markings to prevent friendly-fire incidents.

Italian Medium Tanks

The Italian army did not identify a requirement for medium tanks until the early 1930s. It took until 1936 before Italian industry came up with a suitable candidate vehicle eventually designated the M11/39 medium tank. It took another three years before that medium tank entered into production. The approximately 24,000lb M11/39 had a crew of three. Its 37mm main gun was mounted in its front hull with limited traverse. There was also a small one-man machine-gun-armed turret on the roof of the tank.

By the time production of the M11/39 medium tank ended in 1940, a total of 100 units of the diesel engine-powered tank had been produced. Combat experience with the M11/39 by the Italian army was completely negative with almost every design feature of the tank coming under heavy criticism. This pushed the Italian army to order in 1939 a new medium tank armed with a turret-mounted 47mm main gun. It was to be designated the M13/40 medium tank.

To speed up the design and building of the M13/40 medium tank, Italian industry utilized as much of the M11/39 medium tank as possible. The first production examples of the approximately 31,000lb M13/40 rolled off the assembly lines in 1940. It had a four-man crew and a maximum armour thickness of 40mm.

Like its predecessor, the M13/40 was besieged by a host of serious design flaws, including an under-powered diesel engine. These design flaws greatly reduced the battlefield effectiveness of the vehicle and left it at a decided disadvantage compared to its German medium tank counterparts.

Upgrades

A total of 710 units of the M13/40 were constructed before production ended in favour of a progressively-improved version labelled the M14/41. A total of 695 units of the M14/41 were built between late 1941 and late 1942. The final version of the M13/40 series ordered into production was the M15/42. Despite its similarities to the earlier models, it was both larger and heavier than its predecessor at approximately 35,000lb. Maximum armour thickness remained at 50mm.

The M15/42 was fitted with a new 47mm main gun that had a longer barrel and hence higher muzzle velocity. Only eighty units of the tank were built between 1942 and early 1943 before the Italian army decided that it was obsolete. It was at this point that the Italian army decided to have their industry concentrate on the production of turretless self-propelled guns. The Italian army dropped the weight of its tanks in late 1942 from their designations. This meant the M15/42 became just the M42.

At one point the Italian army was considering having their industry build a near-identical copy of the British army A15 Crusader II tank based on a captured example. An operational prototype was built in early 1943 and named the *Carro M Celere Sahariano*, which translates as 'Medium Saharan Fast Tank'. As the Italian army was no longer engaged in tank combat in North Africa at that time they decided there was no need for the vehicle and all work on the project ended.

Japanese Medium Tanks

The initial medium tank designed and built by Japanese industry was the approximately 25,000lb Type 89 *Yi-Go*. It was armed with a low-velocity 57mm main gun and machine guns. Crew complement was four men. Maximum armour thickness was 17mm. The Type 89 *Yi-Go* entered into limited production in 1931, with full production not commencing until 1933.

By the time production of the Type 89 *Yi-Go* concluded in 1939 a total of 404 units had been built. Of that number, 113 early-production units were gasoline-engine-powered and designated the Type 89A *Yi-Go*. The remaining 291 units were diesel-engine-powered and labelled the Type 89B *Otsu*. The maximum speed of the Type 89 series was 17mph.

The two versions of the Type 89 medium tank series were the mainstay of the Japanese army's armour component during its campaigns in both China and Manchuria between 1937 and 1939. However, by 1935, the Japanese army recognized the growing obsolescence of the Type 89 medium tank series and sought out a replacement.

Next in Line

The search for the Type 89 medium tank replacement eventually led to the fielding of a more advanced medium tank design designated the Type 97 *Chi-Ha*. Production of the approximately 33,000lb diesel-engine-powered tank began in 1938 and ended in 1942 with 1,162 units constructed. It would serve up to the end of the war.

The four-man Type 97 *Chi-Ha* medium tank had the same armament array as the earlier Type 89 medium tank. Maximum armour thickness on the vehicle was 25mm.

A key design feature sought by the Japanese army with the Type 97 *Chi-Ha* was to match the maximum speed of the Type 95 *Ha-Go* light tank on level roads, which was 28mph. To accomplish this goal the Type 97 *Chi-Ha* was fitted with a lengthened version of the suspension system on the Type 95 *Ha-Go* light tank.

Beginning in 1942, Japanese industry began production of a new version of the Type 97 *Chi-Ha* medium tank. It came with a new enlarged turret armed with a high-velocity 47mm main gun. Reflecting this design upgrade it was labelled the Type 97 *Kai Shinhoto Chi-Ha* medium tank. By the time production of the tank was completed in 1943, a total of 930 units had been built. It would serve till the end of the Second World War.

Hungarian Medium Tanks

The Hungarian army began thinking about acquiring a medium tank in 1939. Because time was of the essence and a locally-designed prototype medium tank had failed to meet expectations, it was decided to see if they could obtain a licence to build a suitable foreign-designed medium tank in Hungary. That vehicle turned out to be the Czech medium tank labelled the T21 by its builder. Only a single prototype of the tank had been built in 1938.

Upon testing the T21 prototype in 1940 the Hungarian army decided it met most of their needs. They therefore requested production of an up-armoured version with a maximum armour thickness of 60mm. It was to be armed with a Czech 40mm main gun rather than the original Czech 47mm main gun. That licence-built tank was designated the Turan I by the Hungarian army and entered into service in 1942. A gasoline-powered engine provided the tank with a maximum speed on level roads of 29mph.

Production of the five-man Turan I continued until 1944 with a total of 285 units completed. Combat experience on the Eastern Front quickly demonstrated that the approximately 36,000lb tank was badly outclassed by the Red Army T-34 medium tank series. This would push the Hungarian army to ask the German government for more suitable tanks, which were never supplied in the numbers requested.

(**Opposite, above**) Daimler-Benz built seventy pre-production units of the Panzer III medium tank for testing. The initial pre-production version was the Panzer III Ausf. A pictured here. It was armed with a 37mm main gun designated the KwK 36 L/45. It rode on a suspension system consisting of five large road wheels on either side of the hull individually sprung by coil springs. (*Patton Museum*)

(**Opposite, below**) The coil spring suspension system on the pre-production Panzer III Ausf. A proved unsatisfactory. Daimler-Benz therefore concentrated on the development of a suitable leaf-spring suspension system. It would appear on the Ausf. A through to Ausf. D models of the Panzer III in different design configurations. Pictured is a pre-production Panzer III Ausf. D armed with the 37mm main gun. (*Author's collection*)

(**Above**) The leaf-spring suspension system Daimler-Benz tested on the Panzer III Ausf. B, C and D models did not live up to expectations. This led to the Panzer III series being fitted with six mid-sized road wheels on either side of the hull connected by torsion bars. In this configuration the vehicle was judged a success and it was ordered into production as the Panzer III Ausf. E seen here. (*Patton Museum*)

(**Opposite, above**) The badly-damaged Panzer III Ausf. E pictured here is armed with a 37mm main gun. Visible is the tapered armour cowling projecting out from the gun shield that contained a portion of the main gun recoil system. Visible in the glacis are the two very small openings for the driver's binocular periscopes employed when he was forced to close his armoured visor as is visible in this photograph. (*Author's collection*)

(**Opposite, below**) The Panzer III Ausf. F pictured here is armed with a 37mm main gun. Note the addition of two small cast-armour air intakes on either side of the vehicle's lower two-part stepped glacis. This design feature first appeared on the Ausf. F and was also fitted to all subsequent models of the Panzer III series. It was also eventually retrofitted to Panzer III Ausf. E tanks during factory overhauls. (*Patton Museum*)

An overhead view of a Panzer III Ausf. F armed with a 37mm main gun. The vehicle commander's cupola, which was the same on the pre-production Panzer III Ausf. D and Ausf. E, has horizontal sliding armoured shutters to protect its vision blocks. The screened-over boxes on either side of the rear hull compartment are the air intakes for the engine. (*Patton Museum*)

(**Opposite, above**) As combat experience was gained with the Panzer III Ausf. E and Ausf. F it was clear to the German army that they were under-gunned. This led to the last 100 production units of the Panzer Ausf. F being up-armed with the 50mm KwK 38 L/42 main gun with an external gun shield as seen here. Eventually earlier production units of the tank were armed with the same main gun and external gun shield as they were cycled through factory overhauls. (*Ken Estes*)

(**Opposite, below**) Belonging to a British museum is this restored Panzer III Ausf. F armed with a longer-barrelled 50mm main gun designated KwK 39 L/60. To improve the tank's armour protection levels yet keep the vehicle's weight down, there is spaced armour applied to the turret gun shield and the near-vertical upper front hull plate of the vehicle pictured. (*Tank Museum*)

The gunner's optical sight in a Panzer III Ausf. F is seen in this picture. Also visible is the gunner's manually-operated vertically-oriented elevation hand wheel and below that the gunner's horizontally-oriented manually-operated turret traverse hand wheel. The German army had 348 units of the Panzer III series in service just prior to the invasion of France. (*Patton Museum*)

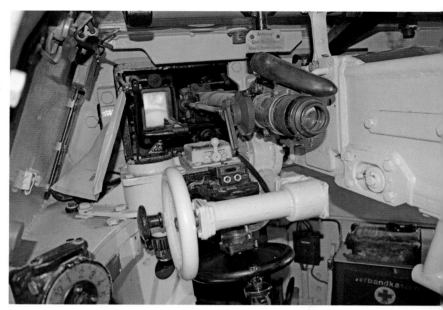

Forming part of the inventory of the US army museum system is this restored Panzer III Ausf. F armed with a 50mm KwK 39 L/60 main gun. It features a horseshoe-shaped spaced-armour arrangement around the sides and rear of its turret. The spaced-armour arrangement of the turret was typically accompanied by spaced-armour plates along either side of the hull. (*Chun-lun Hsu*)

Shown being unloaded upon its arrival in North Africa is a Panzer III Ausf. G. It is armed with a 50mm KwK 38 L/42 main gun. The vertical face of the armoured cowling with four bolts in it contains a portion of the main gun recoil system. It was the same for both the KwK 38 L/42 50mm main gun and the KwK 39 L/60 50mm main guns fitted on the Panzer III series. (*National Archives*)

A stripped Panzer III Ausf. G, armed with a 50mm KwK 38 L/42 main gun, lies abandoned on a North African battlefield. It can be identified as an Ausf. G by the barely-visible ventilation vent on the roof of the turret in front of the commander's cupola. The rear idler design on this vehicle first appeared on the Panzer III Ausf. E. (*Patton Museum*)

(**Opposite, above**) Pictured is a Panzer III Ausf. G armed with the 50mm KwK 38 L/42 main gun. An identifying feature of the Panzer Ausf. E through to Ausf. G was the design of their front hull drive sprockets. A stowage bin at the rear of the turret eventually became a standard feature on the entire Panzer III series. The Ausf. G also came with a new driver vision port design, which was retained on all subsequent models. (*Patton Museum*)

(**Opposite, below**) Captured by the British army in North Africa and returned to England for technical evaluation is this Panzer III Ausf. J. It can be identified as an Ausf. J or a late-production Ausf. H by the new front hull drive sprocket and rear hull idler. These were needed to accommodate wider tracks for the tank to offset the weight imposed by ever-thicker armour applied to the vehicle. (*Patton Museum*)

(**Above**) The Panzer III Ausf. J pictured here featured several new design features not seen on previous models. These included a new armoured ball mount for the upper glacis plate bow machine gun and redesigned lower front hull plate air intake covers. In addition, the towing shackles of earlier versions were replaced by new towing eyes welded to the lower front hull plate. (*Patton Museum*)

(**Opposite, above**) Shown here on display at a US army museum is an early-production Panzer III Ausf. L armed with a 50mm KwK 39 L/60 main gun. It has spaced-armour plates fitted to both the front of its turret as well as the upper glacis plate. This spaced-armour arrangement was retrofitted to earlier versions of the Panzer III series when going through factory overhaul. (*Author's collection*)

(**Opposite, below**) A wartime picture of a Panzer III Ausf. L armed with the 50mm KwK 39 L/60 main gun. An identifying feature of the Ausf. L and subsequent models of the Panzer III series is the lack of turret armoured vision flaps. This particular example of the Ausf. L is an early-production example as it retains the side hull hatches that were discontinued on later production units and follow-on models. (*Patton Museum*)

(**Above**) Shown is a restored Panzer III Ausf. M armed with the 50mm KwK 39 L/60 main gun. With the Ausf. M the smoke-bomb rack mounted on the rear hull of previous versions of the series was discontinued. In its place appeared two three-round smoke grenade discharger units, one mounted on either side of the frontal portion of the turret. (*Thomas Anderson*)

(**Above**) Striking a dramatic pose for the photographer is the vehicle commander of a Panzer III Ausf. M armed with a 75mm KwK 37 L/24 main gun. The Panzer III Ausf. M was not a new production vehicle. Rather it was converted from earlier production models of the Panzer III series, including the Ausf. J and Ausf. L, that were by then obsolete in the tank-killing role. (*Patton Museum*)

(**Opposite, above**) On display at a British museum is this Panzer III Ausf. M armed with a 75mm KwK 37 L/24 main gun. This gun was the original armament of the larger Panzer IV medium tank series. It was optimized for firing high-explosive (HE) rounds at enemy defensive positions and towed anti-tank guns and not for the tank destruction role. The Panzer III Ausf. M would last in front-line service until 1943. (*Patton Museum*)

(**Opposite, below**) Taking part in the German military invasion of Poland in September 1939 is this Panzer IV Ausf. A. It is armed with a 75mm KwK 37 L/24 main gun mounted in an internal gun shield. Krupp-Gruson decided to use a leaf-spring suspension system for the Panzer IV series instead of the yet-to-be-proven torsion bar suspension system chosen by Daimler-Benz for the Panzer III series. (*Patton Museum*)

(**Opposite, above**) Two unique design features of the Panzer IV Ausf. A are seen in this photograph. They include the vehicle commander's drum-style cupola and the driver's small upward armour flap that had also appeared on the pre-production Panzer III Ausf. D. The staggered upper glacis plate pictured would appear on other follow-on versions of the Panzer IV series. (*Patton Museum*)

(**Opposite, below**) On the left-hand side of this photograph is a Panzer IV Ausf. A. Parked next to it is a Panzer IV Ausf. B. It can be recognized as an Ausf. B by several design features: the straight upper hull armour plate, a new vehicle commander's cupola and the armoured visor design for the driver. It retains the internal gun shield of the Ausf. A version of the Panzer IV. (*Patton Museum*)

(**Above**) On campaign in France is a Panzer IV Ausf. B. Unlike the two-piece overhead hatches for the driver and radioman on the Panzer IV Ausf. A, the Panzer IV Ausf. B had single-piece overhead hatches for those front-hull crewmen. The radioman on the Panzer IV Ausf. B was not provided a ball mount for a machine gun. In its place was an open direct-vision port protected by an armoured flap visible in this picture. (*Patton Museum*)

(**Above**) Shown is a Panzer IV Ausf. D during the German invasion of France with a 25mm round having penetrated the vertical lower glacis plate. It, like the previous Panzer IV Ausf. C model, returned to the staggered upper front glacis plate that had first appeared on the Panzer IV Ausf. A. The radioman on the Panzer IV Ausf. D was provided with a ball mount for a machine gun. (*Patton Museum*)

(**Opposite, above**) Shown here on display at a US army museum is this preserved Panzer IV Ausf. D. The suspension system on the Panzer IV series had eight road wheels on each side of the hull. They were paired together in four assemblies. The assemblies were attached to longitudinal twin quarter-elliptic leaf-springs bolted to the hull. (*Christophe Vallier*)

(**Opposite, below**) The Panzer IV Ausf. D pictured had a length of 19ft 5in, a width of 9ft 4in and a height of 8ft 9.5in. On either side of the 75mm KwK 37 L/24 main gun are direct-vision ports for both the gunner and loader protected by armoured flaps. This design feature first appeared on the Panzer IV Ausf. B. (*Patton Museum*)

(**Above**) Visible on the vertical rear hull plate of this Panzer IV Ausf. D is the large cylinder-shaped muffler. Mounted on top of the muffler is a rack containing five smoke bombs. On the Panzer Ausf. D and previous models the vehicle commander's cupola protruded over the rear turret plate as is evident here. (*Patton Museum*)

(**Opposite, above**) Unlike the first three versions of the Panzer IV series that had their 75mm KwK 37 L/42 main gun mounted in an internal gun shield, the same gun on the Panzer IV Ausf. D seen here was mounted in an external gun shield. This came about because combat experience had demonstrated that bullet splash was penetrating the internal gun shields. (*Patton Museum*)

(**Opposite, below**) The bulk of the German army's inventory of the Panzer IV Ausf. D had been lost in combat by 1944. Surviving examples were demoted to the training role. The Panzer IV Ausf. D shown here belongs to a British museum and was up-gunned with a long-barrelled 75mm KwK 40 L/43 main gun. The tank has a length of 19ft 5in, a width of 9ft 4in and a height of 8ft 9.5in. (*Tank Museum*)

(**Opposite, above**) Following the Panzer IV Ausf. D off the production line was the Ausf. E model seen here. It retained the 75mm KwK 37 L/42 main gun in an external gun shield of its predecessor as well as its staggered two-piece upper glacis plate. It did, however, feature a new vehicle commander's cupola shown here that had vertical opened armoured flaps to protect the laminated ballistic glass vision blocks. This was in contrast to the previous model that had horizontal sliding armoured shutters to protect the laminated ballistic glass vision blocks. (*Patton Museum*)

(**Opposite, below**) The next model in the Panzer IV series after the Ausf. E model was the Ausf. F armed with the same 75mm KwK 37 L/42 main gun. When the Ausf. F production run was up-armed with the longer-barrelled KwK 40 L/43 75mm main gun it became the Panzer IV Ausf. G. Note the ball-shaped single-baffle muzzle brake. (*Tank Museum*)

(**Above**) The restored Panzer IV Ausf. G shown here belongs to a German museum. The double-baffle muzzle brake seen on the tank pictured began replacing the original ball-shaped single-baffle muzzle brake in September 1942. The rack on the right-hand side fender was intended for the storage of two spare road wheels and had first appeared on the Ausf. G production line in June 1942. (*Thomas Anderson*)

(**Opposite, above**) Pictured is a Panzer IV Ausf. G belonging to a Russian museum. It lacks the side turret armour vision flaps seen on all previous models in the series. This was a design feature deleted on the Ausf. G production line beginning in April 1942. The original KwK 40 L/43 75mm main gun on the Panzer Ausf. G was replaced with a slightly longer version beginning in April 1943 designated the KwK 40 L/48. (*R. Bazalevsky*)

(**Opposite, below**) On display at a US army museum is this unrestored Panzer IV Ausf. G with the original ball-shaped single-baffle muzzle brake. The horizontal bracket for storing spare track links on the lower front hull of the vehicle began appearing on the Panzer Ausf. G production line in June 1942. (*Author's collection*)

(**Above**) On display at an Israeli museum is a Panzer IV Ausf. G that last saw service with the Syrian army. The upper front glacis plate lacks the cut-out for the two very small circular openings for the driver's binocular periscope seen on all previous Panzer IV series tanks. That design feature had been deleted from the Panzer IV Ausf. G production line beginning in February 1943. (*Vladimir Yakubov*)

(**Opposite, above**) Two features added to the Panzer IV Ausf. G production lines are visible in this photograph. There is the spaced-armour arrangement on the turret and hull, which began appearing on the assembly lines in April 1943. The one-piece hatch fitted to the vehicle commander's cupola began appearing on the Ausf. G production line in February 1943. (*Patton Museum*)

(**Opposite, below**) In this photograph we see the supporting framework for the spaced-armour arrangement that went on to the Panzer IV Ausf. G beginning in April 1943. On the right-hand track fender of the Panzer IV pictured here can be seen the large cylindrical engine pre-filter that was applied to the Panzer IV Ausf. G production line starting in May 1943. (*Patton Museum*)

(**Above**) Shown here is an unrestored Panzer IV Ausf. H that last saw service with the Syrian army. With the addition of spaced armour to the hull sides of the Ausf. H, the driver's right-hand hull side armoured vision flap was discontinued as seen in this photograph. In theory the armoured hatch on this Ausf. H should be one-piece but it is the original two-piece design. (*Author's collection*)

(**Above**) On display at a British historical military vehicle event is this semi-restored Panzer IV Ausf. H. The placement of the vehicle commander's cupola seen on this tank had first appeared on the Panzer IV Ausf. E. On prior models of the Panzer IV series the vehicle commander's cupola was set further back on the turret roof and had resulted in a protrusion at the rear turret plate. (*Ian Wilcox*)

(**Opposite, above**) Belonging to a Swiss museum is this preserved Panzer IV Ausf. H. It differed from the previous model in minor design features. The armour was thickened on the vehicle commander's cupola, the rear turret plate and the front portion of the turret roof. Visible on the front turret roof is the upper portion of an electrically-powered exhaust fan that had first appeared on the Ausf. E. (*Andreas Kirchhoff*)

(**Opposite, below**) The Panzer IV Ausf. J pictured here has in place of the spaced-armour plates applied to the Ausf. G model hull a steel wire mesh counterpart supported by a light steel framework. This feature appeared on the Ausf. J beginning in September 1944. Unlike the Panzer IV series tanks that came before it, the Ausf. J lacked a power traverse system for its turret. (*Patton Museum*)

(**Opposite, above**) On display at a Finnish museum is this preserved Panzer IV Ausf. J. Beginning in May 1944, the pistol ports in the hatches on either side of the turret were discontinued on many production units of the Ausf. J. Visible in this picture are the four all-steel return rollers that had first appeared on the Ausf. H production line in October 1943, in lieu of the former rubber-rimmed road wheels. (*Andreas Kirchhoff*)

(**Above**) On the turret roof of the Panzer IV Ausf. J pictured here can be seen two design features: the uppermost portion of a circular exhaust fan that had first appeared on the Ausf. E, and next to it the uppermost portion of a single-shot grenade-launcher that could be fired by the tank's loader. The latter was capable of firing either anti-personnel grenades or smoke rounds. (*Patton Museum*)

(**Opposite, below**) Part of the collection of a Belgian museum is this preserved Panzer IV Ausf. J. A major external identifying feature of the Ausf. J not visible in this picture was the disposal of the large cylinder-shaped muffler at the rear of the vehicle's hull. This had been a design feature on all previous versions of the Panzer IV series. (*David Marian*)

On the grounds of an Eastern European museum is this unrestored Panzer IV Ausf. J. At peak production, reached in March 1944, German industry turned out 310 units of the Panzer IV series a month. However, by late 1944 into 1945, increasing aerial attacks on German industry were beginning to take their toll. In March 1945, Germany industry built only fifty-five units of the Panzer IV series. *(Thomas Anderson)*

A restored French army Somua S-35 medium tank is pictured at a US army museum. Following the successful German invasion of France in the summer of 1940, approximately 300 units of these were eventually taken into German army service for second-line duties as gun tanks. The vehicle was assigned the German designation Panzer 35S 739(f). *(Christophe Vallier)*

On display at a French museum is a Somua S-35 medium tank armed with a 47mm main gun. Despite some design flaws such as the one-man turret, the German army saw the tank as almost equal to its existing medium tank designs in 1940. The vehicle has a length of 17ft 11in with a width of 6ft 11in and a height of 8ft 1in. (*Christophe Vallier*)

At a German army collection point are a number of captured Red Army T-34 medium tanks. Despite thousands of T-34 tanks falling into German army hands in various states of condition between 1941 and 1943, most went off to the smelters in Germany. A very small number were retained as gun tanks by the German army, typically in secondary roles. (*Patton Museum*)

All the captured Red Army T-34 tanks that were employed by the German army against their former owners were identified with a variety of large German military markings as seen in this photograph. Based on pictorial evidence, a few were fitted with the vehicle commander's cupola from destroyed German Panzer III and IV tanks. (*Patton Museum*)

(**Opposite, above**) In 1939, the Italian army took into service the M11/39 medium tank pictured here somewhere in North Africa. It was, to all intents and purposes, simply an enlarged version of the CV-33 light tank series. The increase in size allowed for the fitting of a 37mm main gun in the front hull and a one-man turret armed with two machine guns. (*Tank Museum*)

(**Opposite, below**) The Italian army was well aware of the design limitations of the M11/39 medium tank and pushed Italian industry for something better. What they got in 1940 was the M13/40 medium tank armed with a turret-mounted 47mm main gun. The example pictured here is on display at a US army museum. Crew size could vary from three to four men. (*Author's collection*)

(**Opposite, above**) Pictured is an abandoned Italian army M13/40 medium tank. The suspension system and tracks of the M13/40 were the same as those of its predecessor, the M11/39. Radios did not appear on the M13/40 until the middle of 1941. Vehicle length was 16ft 2in with a width of 7ft 3in and a height of 7ft 10in. (*Tank Museum*)

(**Above**) Compared to the German army medium tanks in service in 1940 and 1941, the Italian army M13/40 was clearly inferior. However, compared to the British tanks employed during the early fighting in North Africa it was not that far inferior. This meant that when examples of the M13/40 were captured they were sometimes pressed into service as seen here with an example marked with large kangaroos. (*Tank Museum*)

(**Opposite, below**) On display at a Canadian museum is this Italian-designed and built M13/40 medium tank. It was followed off the production line by the slightly-improved M14/41. The main reason for the Italian army's inability to field more effective medium tanks during the Second World War was the immaturity of Italian industry at the time. (*Paul and Loren Hannah*)

There was a redesigned version of the M14/41 placed into service by the Italian army assigned the designation M15/42, an example of which is seen here on display at a French museum. Only ninety units of the M15/42 entered into Italian army service beginning in January 1943. Upon the Italian surrender these vehicles and twenty-eight newly-built units were taken into German army service. (*Christophe Vallier*)

Pictured is a gasoline-engine-powered Japanese army medium tank designated the Type 89A *I-Go*. The tank had originally been envisioned as a light tank but continuing weight growth resulted in the Japanese army relabelling it as a medium tank. The 57mm main gun was of very low muzzle velocity and only suitable for the destruction of enemy defensive positions, not of opposing tanks. (*Tank Museum*)

On display at a US army museum is a Japanese army Type 89B *I-Go* medium tank. The prefix letter 'B' in the designation reflects it being diesel-engine-powered. The tank has a length of 14ft 1in, a width of 7ft and a height of 7ft 2in. It had an operational range of approximately 100 miles. *(Richard Hunnicutt)*

The Japanese army replacement for the Type 89 *I-Go* medium tank series was the Type 97 *Chi-Ha* seen here. It is from the initial production lot as it is armed with the same low-velocity 57mm main gun that was mounted in the Type 89 *I-Go* medium tank series. The tank's diesel engine provided it with an operational range of approximately 130 miles. *(National Archives)*

功臣号坦克（日本1937年造）
MERIT TANK. MADE IN JAPAN IN 1937

A wartime image of a Type 97 *Kai Shinhoto Chi-Ha* medium tank. In contrast to other medium tanks of the Second World War the driver's position was located on the right-hand side of the tank's front hull and the bow gunner on the left side of the front hull. Note that the driver lacked an overhead hatch. (*Patton Museum*)

(**Opposite, above**) The Japanese army was not unaware that the low-velocity 57mm main gun on the Type 97 *Chi-Ha* medium tank was not optimized for the anti-tank role. This led to a redesigned and up-gunned version seen here at a US army museum labelled the Type 97 *Kai Shinhoto Chi-Ha*. It featured an enlarged turret armed with a high-velocity 47mm main gun. (*Richard Hunnicutt*)

(**Opposite, below**) On display at a Chinese museum is an example of the Type 97 *Kai Shinhoto Chi-Ha* medium tank. A great many captured examples of the tank were employed by the Red Chinese army in the immediate post-war period. The Type 97 *Kai Shinhoto Chi-Ha* has a length of 18ft 1in, a width of 7ft 8in and a height of 7ft 4in. (*Paul and Loren Hannah*)

In 1940, the German army provided the Hungarian army with two prototypes of a pre-war Czech-designed medium tank labelled the T-T21. It had not been accepted by the Czech army for service. Hungarian industry copied and modified the design and built the *Turan* I seen here armed with a 40mm main gun. (*Charles Kliment collection*)

The Hungarian army *Turan* I medium tank pictured here was powered by a gasoline engine that provided it with an operational range of approximately 102 miles. It was 18ft 2in in length, 8ft wide and 7ft 10in high. Like the German army Panzer IV medium tank, it had side turret doors for the crew and rode on a leaf-spring-based suspension system. (*Charles Kliment collection*)

Chapter Three

Late-War Medium Tanks

Despite some unexpected shortcomings in the armour protection level and armament of its Panzer III and Panzer IV medium tanks discovered during the conquest of France, the German army remained extremely confident that its tanks would prevail over their more numerous Red Army counterparts during the invasion of the Soviet Union planned for the summer of 1941.

Much to the surprise of the German army, it was discovered in the opening stages of the invasion of the Soviet Union that the frontal armour on the Red Army's T-34 medium tanks and their KV-1 heavy tanks was immune to all their existing tank and anti-tank guns; worse was the fact that the 76.2mm main guns fitted to both Red Army tanks easily penetrated the frontal armour on German medium tanks.

Of the two Red Army tanks that had caused such consternation to the German army it was the T-34 that most concerned them. The senior leadership of the German army quickly alerted the German Armament Ministry to the danger posed by this new Red Army tank. At the same time, the question was being asked as to how the German Armament Ministry had allowed the technical superiority of German tanks to be lost.

A Solution

After their evaluation of a captured Red Army T-34, the German Armament Ministry staff decided that a new medium tank was needed for the German army. Some had suggested that the quickest way to meet the threat posed by the T-34 was to merely come up with a German-designed and built inspired copy, which is what Daimler-Benz decided upon.

After a great deal of meddling by Hitler, who had preferred the Daimler-Benz design, the German army's Ordnance Department eventually selected MAN to design and build the chassis of a medium tank and Rheinmetall-Borsig AG the turret. The 75mm main gun chosen for the new medium tank was designated the 7.5cm KwK 42 L/70 and was also designed and built by Rheinmetall-Borsig AG.

Designations

The German army ordered pilots of the new medium tank chassis from MAN on 15 May 1942. They were assigned the designation Panzer V Panther Ausf. D. On

Hitler's orders the designation prefix 'Panzer V' was phased out in February 1944. The vehicle's ordnance inventory number was 171.

The name 'Panther' came from the Panther Commission, the small group of tank designers and engineers that had set the design requirements for the vehicle. In most cases Western Allied wartime documents generally refer to the Panther tank as the 'Mark V'.

Rushed into Service

In August 1942, MAN presented the German army with two pilots of the Panther Ausf. D for testing: one had a turret fitted and the other did not. In spite of numerous design shortcomings, the tank was ordered into production in November 1942. Hitler badly wanted them for a major offensive operation on the Eastern Front planned for the summer of 1943 and assigned the name Operation CITADEL.

The Panther Ausf. D introduction into combat during Operation CITADEL in early July 1943 was a major disappointment. Besides their mechanical immaturity that rendered the majority of the 200 units amassed for the operation unfit for combat after the first few days of fighting, the tank battalions that had been equipped with them proved insufficiently trained. This led to too many Panther Ausf. Ds being lost in combat due to poor tactical handling.

Different Models

By the time production of the Panther Ausf. D ended in September 1943 a total of 850 units had been constructed. Feedback from the user community and industry-inspired improvements led to the manufacture of an improved Ausf. A model beginning in September 1943. The reasoning for the out-of-sequence letter suffix in the vehicle's designation remains unknown. When production of the Panther Ausf. A concluded in September 1943 a total of 2,200 units had rolled off the assembly lines.

The replacement for the Panther Ausf. A was the Panther Ausf. G with the first examples coming off the factory floor in the spring of 1944. It would turn out to be the most numerous model of the Panther tank series built, with German documents showing that at least 2,943 units were assembled, as with the previous version by a number of different firms. The replacement for the Panther Ausf. G was to be the much-redesigned Panther Ausf. F model but the war in Europe ended before production could commence.

Firepower

One of the few positive points of feedback that came out of the Panther Ausf. D's introduction into combat during Operation CITADEL was the effectiveness of its 75mm main gun. During the fighting it was reported that Panther Ausf. D gunners were consistently destroying Red Army T-34 medium tanks at ranges up to

2,188 yards. On a number of occasions, they engaged and destroyed them at the unheard-of range of up to 3,282 yards.

The standard APCBC-HE round for the Panther tank's main gun weighed 31lb, with the projectile portion of the round being approximately 16lb. When it left the 75mm main gun barrel it was travelling at more than 3,000 ft/sec. This high muzzle velocity resulted in its ability to penetrate 112mm of armour at a range of 1,094 yards and 88mm of armour at 2,188 yards.

A German POW told his captors that Panther tank gunners were trained to engage American M4 series medium tanks without hesitation at ranges anywhere between 2,000 to 2,200 yards. Accuracy testing by the US army on captured German Panther tanks showed that at 1,000 yards its main gun could place all its shots within a 12-in circle. In an extract from a March 1945 US army report appears this quote from Sergeant Leo Anderson of the 2nd Armored Division recounting a single engagement his unit had with two Panther tanks:

> Our column was advancing towards its objective when suddenly we began to draw direct fire from German tanks … we located two Mark V tanks at about 2,800 to 3,000 yards. At once our tank destroyers and tanks opened fire on them. The gunners had the eye to hit them but our guns didn't have the power to knock them out … The Jerries' gun didn't fail, they knocked out three of our tank destroyers and one Sherman tank at 2,800 to 3,000 yards. If our tanks had been as good as the German tanks they would never have scored a hit.

The Panther's main gun could also fire a Gr. 40 round, which had a muzzle velocity of 3,937 ft/sec. At a range of 1,094 yards it could penetrate 149mm of armour. When the range went up to 2,188 yards it could punch through 106mm of armour. Besides their AP rounds, the Panther tank series also carried an HE round that had a muzzle velocity of 2,300 ft/sec.

Ammunition Storage

The first two production versions of the Panther tank series had authorized storage for seventy-nine main gun rounds. The Panther Ausf. G had authorized storage for eighty-two main gun rounds. As with all the Axis and Allied tank crews, there was both the authorized storage for their vehicles and what they really stuffed into them.

According to a British army report dated December 1944, a captured German tanker stated the following regarding the main gun ammunition storage arrangement of Panther tanks then in service:

> Standard instructions are that 120 rounds for the 7.5cm gun and 3,350 rounds for each MG should be stored in the Panther before going into action. It is left to the crew to decide on the proportion of AP and HE shells to be carried; normally the proportion should be 50 per cent of each. [The] prisoner of war

carried 9,000 rounds of MG ammo for his two MGs. Stowage space is provided for 79 rounds of 7.5cm ammo. The extra 41 rounds are added by removing the rack from ammo boxes and by carrying some rounds in the spent cartridge box … under the recoil guard. No rounds are carried on the floor.

Crew Positions

The Panther tank series was serviced by five men, as had been the Panzer III and Panzer IV medium tank series. This comprised the tank commander, gunner, loader, driver and radio-operator. The tank commander position on the Panther tank series was on the left-hand side of the main gun recoil guard towards the rear of the turret, with the gunner directly in front and below him.

The Panther's loader's position was on the right-hand side of the main gun. He had no overhead hatch. His ingress and egress from the tank was only by way of a small hatch in the rear turret wall plate. A 1947 British army report had this to say about his work space: 'A seat was optional. As the height of the turret is only 5 feet 3 inches a loader of normal height must stoop. The combination of these factors was certain to result in fatigue, especially if the vehicles were on the move for long periods.'

The Panther tank driver sat in the left front hull of the vehicle and steered the vehicle with two levers, one on either side of his seat. A US army soldier who drove a captured Panther tank commented in a March 1945 report on the ease of steering the vehicle: 'Boosters on the steering laterals of a Mark V [Panther] make it much easier to drive them than our tanks.'

On the Panther Ausf. D and Ausf. A the driver was not provided with the option of operating the vehicle 'opened up', with his head and upper torso projecting out over the front hull roof. His overhead hatch, as with that of the radioman that sat opposite him in the front hull, was only intended for ingress and egress. For whatever reason, maybe based on user input, the driver of the Panther Ausf. G was provided with the option of operating the vehicle opened up.

Turret Protection

The turrets on the three production model Panther tanks featured a curved gun shield that extended across almost the entire width of the turret front and ranged in thickness from 100mm to 110mm. The front turret wall behind the gun shield was 100mm thick. On the unfielded Panther Ausf. F the turret was much smaller and had a rounded 150mm thick gun shield.

A design weakness of the production Panther tank gun shields identified in combat was the occasional loss of a tank because an enemy AP projectile struck below the apex of its curved gun shield. When this occurred, the enemy projectile was deflected downward through the thin roof armour of the tank's hull into the driver/radioman's compartment.

To address the problem of projectiles being directed into the driver/radioman's compartment by the Panther tank's curved gun shield, German industry applied two design fixes. The first was the thickening of the armour over the driver/radioman's compartment on the Panther Ausf. G. Second, some Panther Ausf. G tanks were fitted at the factory with a modified version of the original gun shield that had a chin-like protrusion on its bottommost portion. This was intended to deflect incoming projectiles upwards rather than downwards.

The sides and rear of the production Panther tank turrets were 45mm thick and sloped at 24 degrees. Their roof armour was only 17mm thick. On the unfielded Panther Ausf. F the turret roof was 40mm thick and the 25-degree sloped turret walls were 60mm thick.

Frontal Protection

Always the strong point of the Panther tank series was its 80mm thick glacis plate sloped at 55 degrees. This fact was first demonstrated during Operation CITADEL when it resisted penetration by both the 76.2mm main guns on the T-34 medium tanks and KV-1 heavy tanks at normal combat ranges, as well as the Red Army's existing towed anti-tank gun inventory. At one point the German army had considered a 100mm thick glacis for the Panther tank series but that proved unworkable.

In a 1944 British army report there appears this confirmation of the survivability of the Panther's glacis plate:

> While the armour of the Panther is less thick than that of the Tiger [E], the use of sloped armour at high angles gives it a very good degree of protection. The hull front is immune to 6-pounder [57mm] at all ranges and can only be defeated by the 17-pdr [76.2mm] gun under very restricted conditions.

The downside of the 80mm glacis plate on the Panther tank series was the fact that the vehicle was originally designed to have only a 60mm glacis plate. The vehicle's powertrain had not been designed to handle the extra weight that came with the thicker glacis plate. As there was no time to redesign the now approximately 100,000lb vehicle to support the extra weight, the tank would be plagued by serious reliability problems with its powertrain throughout its short service life.

Side Hull and Turret Protection

The lower hull sides of all three production models of the Panther tank were vertical and 40mm thick, with additional protection being provided by the vehicle's large overlapping road wheels. The superstructure sides of the first two production versions were 40mm thick and sloped at 40 degrees. Affixed to the rear bottom portion of the superstructure sides of the first two production versions of the Panther tank was a tapered 40mm thick vertical piece of armour.

To speed up production of the Panther tank Ausf. G it was decided by German industry that it was to be built with single-piece superstructure side plates sloped at 29 degrees. As the slope for the new one-piece superstructure plates on the Panther Ausf. G was less than that on two previous versions of the Panther tank it was thickened to 50mm to compensate.

The German army was always concerned about the relatively thin superstructure armour side plates and turret sides of its Panther tanks. They therefore stressed to their crews the need to be aware of them in combat. This design feature was commented upon in a British army report dated 24 May 1944: 'The hull and turret sides of Panther, even having regard to the up-armouring of the front at their expense appears weaker than would have been expected in a tank of its weight.'

As with the Panzer III and Panzer IV medium tanks the Panther tank series, beginning with the Panther Ausf. D, was fitted with spaced armour plates. Unlike the previous medium tanks that had them both for the turret and lower hull/super-structure, those fitted to the Panther tank series only covered a portion of the upper suspension system and hull.

The bottom hull plate of the Panther Ausf. D hull was only 16mm thick. Some-time during the production of the Panther Ausf. A it was thickened at the front to 30mm to minimize anti-tank mine damage. This design change was continued on the Panther Ausf. G.

The British army concluded after testing captured Panther tanks that a single anti-tank mine going off under a track of the tank would immobilize it. Two going off simultaneously under the inner edge of track would rupture the bottom hull plate of the Panther tank.

Suspension System

The Panther tank suspension consisted of large overlapping road wheels supported by transversely-mounted high-strength steel torsion bars spanning the bottom of the vehicle's hull. Torsion bar suspension systems and large overlapping road wheels had first appeared on pre-Second World War German army half-track designs in the 1930s.

The large overlapping road wheel configuration on the Panther tank and its wide steel tracks offered a very even distribution of load along its length, thus contributing to lower ground pressure. Ground pressure or 'flotation' is the ratio of a tank's weight to the surface area supported by its tracks. The lower the ground pressure, the greater a tank's ability to cross over soft terrain.

Despite the much greater weight of the Panther tank compared to the American M4 series of medium tanks, it had equal or superior off-road mobility as attested to by Technical Sergeant Willard D. May of the 2nd Armored Division in a March 1945 report: 'I have taken instruction on the Mark V [Panther] and have found, first, it is easily as maneuverable as the Sherman; second, the flotation exceeds that of the Sherman.'

The downside of the large overlapping road wheels configuration on the Panther tank included mud packing tightly between the road wheels at night during the winter months and then freezing. This would immobilize the tank the following morning, requiring the crew to dislodge the ice with a variety of tools including picks and crossbars.

Another disadvantage of the Panther tank's suspension system was lower track life due to the continual side-to-side movement of the tracks over the many road wheels. There was also the difficulty in replacing individual road wheels when damaged, especially those closer to the lower hull sides.

Powertrain Issues

Analysis of captured Panther tanks and statements by their crews convinced the British army that the vehicle's transmission entered into production without adequate development and testing. The late Jacques Littlefield, who both funded and supervised the restoration of a Panther Ausf. A, made these comments on his impressions of the vehicle's transmission: 'It's not a badly-designed system or overly complex the way other systems on the Panther are. It's designed to be compact, efficient, and easy to shift. However, it is certainly not designed for maintenance in the field.'

Soon after the introduction of the Panther Ausf. D into field use the vehicle's steering units began exhibiting reliability problems. The steering units of the Panther tank formed part of the tank's transmission unit and were a double-differential type, with auxiliary skid brakes.

After the Second World War German tank designers informed their British army captors that they were well aware of the problem with the tank's steering units but felt it was not that serious an issue because the transmission would normally fail prior to the steering unit.

The British army had also concluded that the Panther's final drive units were poorly-designed and prone to failure due to manufacturing defects. Jacques Littlefield had this to say about the tank's final drive units:

> When we tested ours, the alloy and the strength of these particular gears was as good as what we could make them from today … Part of the problem with the final drives was no doubt due to the vehicle's growth in weight … I'm going to guess that what ended up happening with the final drives is that they were designed for the lower weight vehicle, and there wasn't the physical size [available] to where you could make the gears wider and stronger. Since they weren't able to make them wider, they just left them the way they were originally designed.

Dr Wolfgang Sterner, a late-war Panther Ausf. G tank commander, sums up his impressions of the vehicle's mechanical problems:

> I was assigned to the Panzer Lehr Division in January 1945. However, by this time problems with the Panther were not so dramatic anymore, because at that time many things had been improved ... We still had technical problems with the Panther, but not much more than with the Mark IV [medium tank]. On the other hand, we never had any problems with the tactical fighting capabilities of the Panther; in my opinion it was outstanding.

Engine Issues

The majority of Panther tanks were powered by the Maybach HL 230 P30 gasoline engine that produced 700hp at 3,000rpm. A serious problem with this engine was its propensity to spontaneously burst into flame due to some design shortcomings. Shortly after the Second World War, the British army brought back to Great Britain a number of Panther Ausf. G tanks for testing. The final test report noted their constant tendency to have engine compartment fires.

Charles Lemon, a former curator at the now-closed Patton Museum of Armor and Cavalry, had this to say about the Panther tank's engine compartment fire problems:

> The Panther was one of those vehicles that was a very unforgiving vehicle for a novice driver. If you pushed the gas at just the wrong time at the wrong place, it would backfire out of the engine and catch fire, and you were basically sitting in a very large target.

Japanese Medium Tanks

By 1941, the Japanese army was aware that its pre-war-designed medium tanks were badly under-armoured. This led to the design of an up-armoured version of the Type 97 *Kai Shinhoto Chi-Ha* medium tank. The up-armoured model had a maximum armour thickness of 50mm and was designated the Type 1 *Chi-He*.

To compensate for the extra weight of the Type 1 *Chi-He* due to the thicker armour, it was fitted with a more powerful diesel engine. Only 170 units of the medium tank were built between 1943 and 1945. All were retained in Japan and therefore saw no combat.

In an effort produce a medium tank with a main gun optimized to fire an HE round of a sufficient size, Japanese industry took the turret of the Type 97 *Kai Shinhoto Chi-Ha* medium tank and rearmed it with a short-barrelled 75mm main gun. They mounted that modified turret on the chassis of the Type 1 *Chi-He* medium tank. This mix-match of components was referred to as the Type 2 *Ho-I* medium tank. Only thirty-one units were built between 1944 and 1945 with none of them leaving Japan.

Up-Gunned Versions

Upon learning of the existence of the better-armed and armoured American M4 series medium tanks in 1943, the Japanese army decided as a stop-gap to take a modified and lengthened Type 1 *Chi-He* chassis and mount upon it a newly-designed turret armed with a long-barrelled, high-velocity 75mm main gun. This interim tank was accepted for service in 1943 and designated the Type 3 *Chi-Nu* medium tank.

As production of the Type 3 *Chi-Nu* medium tank did not begin until 1944 and Japanese industry was suffering badly under American bombing raids by this time, only thirty-one units of the tank were built. All were retained for defence of the Japanese homeland in case of the Allied invasion that never occurred.

There was another attempt at fielding a more modern medium tank assigned the designation Type 4 *Chi-To*. Both larger and more heavily armoured than the Type 3 *Chi-Nu* medium tank, only two units were completed before the Japanese surrender. Like the Type 3 *Chi-Nu* medium tank, the Type 4 *Chi-To* medium tank was armed with a long-barrelled, high-velocity 75mm main gun. The maximum armour thickness on the tank was 75mm.

The follow-on to the Type 4 *Chi-To* medium tank was the Type 5 *Chi-Ri* medium tank armed with a Japanese-designed and built 88mm main gun. Only a single prototype of this tank was ever completed and was found by the US army during its post-war occupation of Japan.

The sole surviving example of a Panther Ausf. D is seen here preserved as a monument tank in Western Europe. Visible on the turret side is a large circular communication port that allowed the vehicle commander to talk to those outside the tank. The communication port would be discontinued on the Ausf. D production line beginning in July 1943. *(Pierre-Olivier Buan)*

A design feature for the entire production run of the Panther Ausf. D is the drum-shaped vehicle commander's cupola seen in this illustration. It was approximately 10in in height and had six direct-vision apertures protected by laminated ballistic glass. Also seen in the illustration are the two three-round smoke grenade-launchers on the front of the turret that were quickly discontinued. (*George Bradford*)

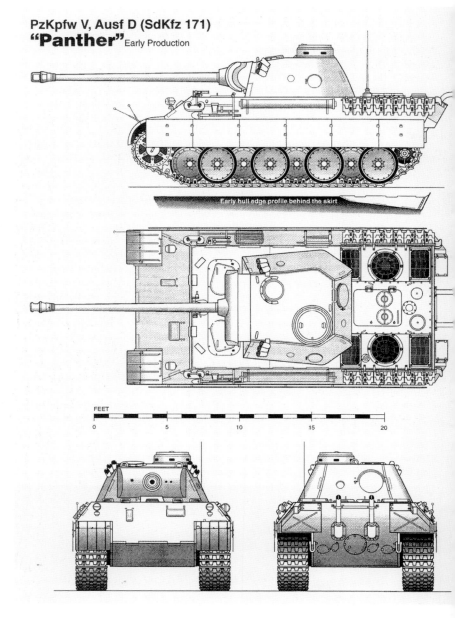

PzKpfw V, Ausf D (SdKfz 171)
"Panther" Early Production

Early hull edge profile behind the skirt

FEET

0   5   10   15   20

(**Opposite, above**) When under fire the vehicle commander on the Panther Ausf. D could protect the six laminated ballistic glass blocks of his drum-shaped cupola with an interior rotating armour ring. Visible in this picture is the loader's rear turret hatch of an Ausf. D as well as two of the three plugged turret pistol ports known in the German language as the *MP Stophen*. (*Virginia Museum of Military Vehicles*)

(**Opposite, below**) This picture is of the Panther tank loader's rear turret wall hatch, a design feature common to the entire series. Besides using it to enter and leave the vehicle, the loader would employ it to upload main gun ammunition. In combat, the Panther tank loader would often leave it partially open so that he could hurl spent main gun cartridge cases out of the tank. (*David T. Lin*)

(**Above**) A feature on the entire Panther Ausf. D production run and the early-production units of a subsequent version was a small upward-opening armoured flap on the right-hand side of the glacis. It served as the radioman's pistol port. Note the two small apertures on the right-hand side of the gun shield for the gunner's binocular gun sight. (*Virginia Museum of Military Vehicles*)

(**Opposite, above**) From the radioman's position looking forward can be seen the opening mechanism for the small upward-opening armour flap in the glacis that had first appeared on the Panther Ausf. D. Like the pistol ports in the Panther Ausf. D turret, it would allow the radioman to aim and fire an onboard weapon (pistol/submachine gun) at close-in enemy infantry. (*David Marian*)

(**Opposite, below**) Allied soldiers are examining a derelict Panther Ausf. D in this photograph. Visible are the two storage bins located on either side of the rear hull plate. This would be a feature seen on all succeeding models of the Panther series. Missing from the rear of this vehicle is a horizontally-stored jack for replacing damaged road wheels. Visible are the two identical engine exhaust manifold pipes. (*Author's collection*)

The metal bar extending out from the breech of this prototype Panther tank's 75mm main gun is a recoil guard. On the left-hand side of this image can be seen the vehicle commander's seat and the interior components of one of three pistol ports that appeared on the Panther Ausf. D. Early-production units of a follow-on model retained only a single pistol port on the right-hand side of the turret. (*Tank Museum*)

A ghosted illustration of the turret from a Panther Ausf. D. On the bottom of the turret basket floor, under the breech of the main gun, is the spent cartridge case bin. Upon a round being fired, the cartridge case was ejected rearwards and impacted with a leather pad located at the inside rear of the recoil guard (not shown). It then dropped down into the spent cartridge case bin.

(*Patton Museum*)

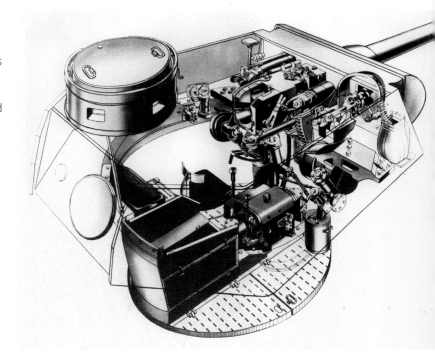

In this picture taken from the loader's position on a Panther Ausf. D can be seen the loader's hatch and the interior components of a rear turret wall pistol port. Visible at the uppermost portion of the photograph is a hand wheel employed by the vehicle commander to close an interior armoured ring to protect the cupola's six laminated ballistic glass blocks. (*Patton Museum*)

The Panther Ausf. Ds pictured are early-production units as indicated by the two front headlights. Later production models had only a single front headlight. Even before the first Panther Ausf. D rolled off the factory floor, there was some thought given to the production of a more heavily-armoured version assigned the designation Panther II. By the summer of 1943, interest had waned in the vehicle and developmental work ceased. (*National Archives*)

The Panther Ausf. D shown here came with a single-speed, hydraulic-powered turret traverse system that took sixty seconds to rotate the turret 360 degrees. By way of comparison, the variable electro-hydraulic-powered turret traverse system on the first generation of most M4 series medium tanks armed with a 75mm main gun could be rotated 360 degrees in just fifteen seconds. (*Patton Museum*)

The majority of road wheels on this Panther Ausf. D are of the original design with sixteen rim bolts arrayed around their circumference. Some had extra rivets applied at the factory to strengthen them as is the case with the centre rear road wheel seen in this picture. Eventually a road wheel with twenty-four rim bolts began appearing on the Ausf. D production line in August 1943. (*Virginia Museum of Military Vehicles*)

This illustration from a Panther manual shows the suspension system. The twisting action of the torsion bars pushed down on the road wheels to keep them on the ground. To prevent the torsion bar spring action from pitching or oscillating the vehicle, the suspension system had four shock absorbers (shock dampers) as seen in this illustration. (*English translation by James D. Brown*)

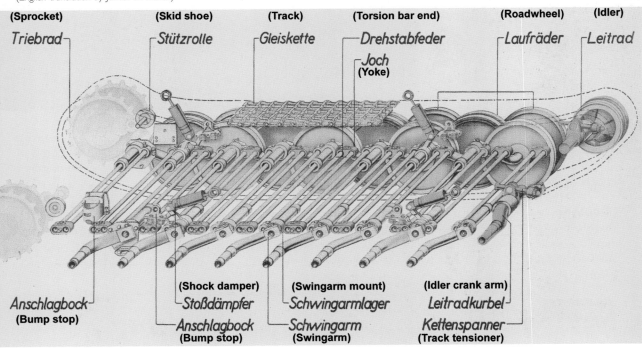

(Sprocket) Triebrad

(Skid shoe) Stützrolle

(Track) Gleiskette

(Torsion bar end) Drehstabfeder

Joch (Yoke)

(Roadwheel) Laufräder

(Idler) Leitrad

Anschlagbock (Bump stop)

(Shock damper) Stoßdämpfer

Anschlagbock (Bump stop)

(Swingarm mount) Schwingarmlager

Schwingarm (Swingarm)

(Idler crank arm) Leitradkurbel

Kettenspanner (Track tensioner)

A factory shot of a Panther Ausf. D assembly line with very early production units evident by the twin headlights on either side of their glacis. Later production units of the Ausf. D had only a single headlight mounted on the glacis as a cost-saving measure. Early-production Ausf. D units were plagued by serious quality control issues due to the rush to put them into production without sufficient testing. (*Patton Museum*)

(**Opposite, above**) For whatever reason this Panther Ausf. D is missing its outer set of road wheels. This particular vehicle could be mistaken for an early-production unit of the follow-on model. The only feature that positively identifies it as a Panther Ausf. D is the pistol port visible on the right-hand side turret plate. This feature does not appear on the turrets of subsequent models in the Panther series. (*National Archives*)

(**Opposite, below**) Despite the Panther Ausf. D being replaced on the assembly line by two successively-improved models, it would linger in service until the end of the war in Europe in ever-declining numbers. Pictured is a Panther Ausf. D in early 1945 that had either been knocked out or abandoned for mechanical reasons. Lack of fuel was also a late-war issue that could sideline German tanks. (*National Archives*)

(**Above**) Following the Panther Ausf. D off the production line was the progressively-improved Panther Ausf. A. A destroyed example is seen here. It involved mounting a redesigned and upgraded Panther tank turret on a modified chassis of the earlier Panther Ausf. D. An external feature that is commonly employed to identify the Ausf. A is the design of the new vehicle commander's cupola visible in this photograph. (*Patton Museum*)

(**Opposite, above**) The new vehicle commander's cupola of the Panther Ausf. A and a follow-on model is shown here. It was of cast-armour construction and contained seven periscopes arranged around its circumference protected by armoured hoods. Pictorial evidence shows that some of the drum-shaped vehicle commander's cupolas of the Ausf. D were also fitted to early-production Ausf. A tanks. (*Andreas Kirchhoff*)

(**Opposite, below**) Beginning in November or December 1943, the small armour flap in the glacis of early-production Panther Ausf. A tanks was done away with. In its place was a new spherical cast-armoured ball mount armed with a machine gun as seen here. In the German language this new machine gun mount, which contained an optical sight, was known as the *Kugelblende*. (*Author's collection*)

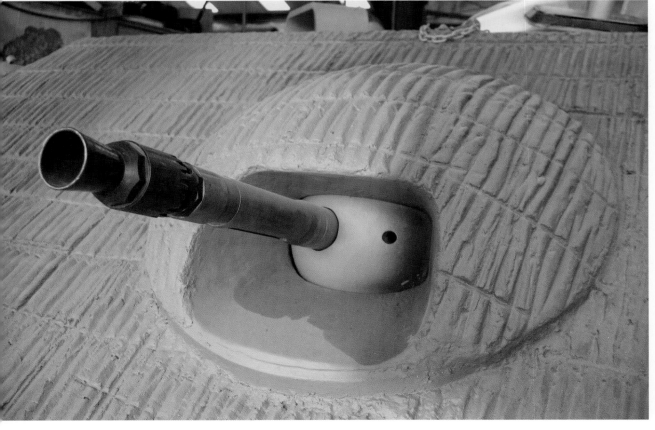

(**Above**) This knocked-out Panther Ausf. A is a later-production example as it has the machine-gun-armed spherical cast-armoured ball mount in the glacis. Note that the road wheels are of the second-generation type with twenty-four rim bolts rather than the sixteen on the original design. With its main guns pointed forward the tank was 29ft long. It had a width of 10ft 9in and a height of 10ft 2in. (*Patton Museum*)

(**Opposite, above**) In this picture we see the radioman's position on a restored Panther Ausf. A. In front of his seat are the mount and sight for the glacis-mounted machine gun. With the American M4 series of medium tanks the glacis-mounted machine-gun mount had no optical sight. The bow gunner relied on watching the tracers from his overhead periscope to direct his fire. (*Author's collection*)

(**Opposite, below**) On display at a French army base is this restored Panther Ausf. A. The *Zimmerit* (anti-magnetic coating) on the tank began showing up on the Ausf. D production lines in April 1943 and the Ausf. A assembly lines in August or early September 1943. The monocular gun sight aperture in the right-hand side of the gun shield appeared on the Ausf. A assembly lines beginning in late 1943. (*Pierre-Olivier Buan*)

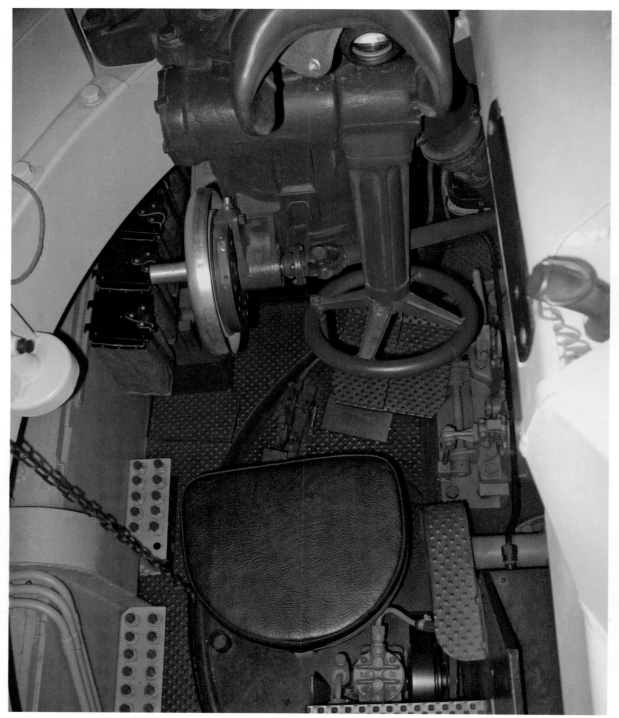

Looking down into the turret of a restored Panther Ausf. A shows the seat and controls for the gunner. At the very top of the picture is the leather brow-piece for a monocular gun sight. The vertically-oriented hand wheel is for manually elevating or depressing the main gun, with the horizontally-oriented hand wheel for manually traversing the main gun. (*Author's collection*)

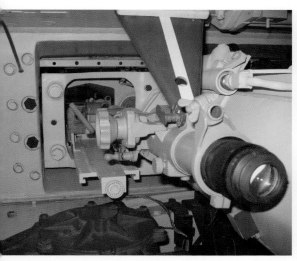 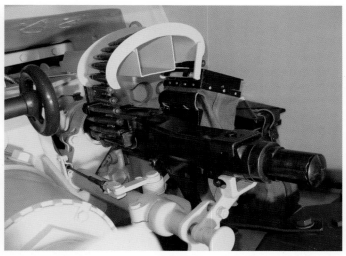

(**Above, left**) Shown inside a restored Panther Ausf. A is the gunner's monocular gun sight designated the TZF 12a. It has dual magnification: 2.5-power and 5-power. The gunner's leather brow-piece is missing in this picture. The previous binocular gun sight on the Panther Ausf. D and early-production Panther Ausf. A was labelled the TZF 12. (*Author's collection*)

(**Above, right**) In this picture we see the coaxial machine gun in a restored Panther Ausf. A. It was located on the right-hand side of the vehicle's turret and serviced by the loader. The gunner was responsible for aiming and firing the coaxial machine gun. The spent cartridge cases dropped into a metal box directly below the weapon. (*David Marian*)

(**Below**) Belonging to the collection of a French museum is this restored Panther Ausf. A. The circular steel bar on the top of the vehicle commander's cupola began appearing on the Ausf. A assembly lines in August 1943. It was for the mounting of a machine gun. On the Ausf. A the turret front armour plate was fitted to the rest of the turret by squared-off joints. On the Ausf. D these joints were dove-tailed. (*David T. Lin*)

(**Above**) The driver's direct vision port in the glacis of a restored Panther Ausf. A. The laminated ballistic glass block was replaceable. Unlike the drivers on modern tanks equipped with power steering, Panther tank drivers were forced to deal with a single fixed-radius controlled-differential steering system, which offered them only seven fixed-radius turn possibilities. (*Author's collection*)

(**Opposite, above**) The driver's position on a restored Panther Ausf. A. At the uppermost portion of the photograph are the interior components of the driver's glacis-mounted direct vision port. To the left of his seat is storage space for four main gun rounds. On the right is the driver's instrument panel mounted on the transmission housing. (*Author's collection*)

(**Opposite, below**) If battlefield conditions dictated, the drivers of the Panther Ausf. D and Ausf. A would close the hinged armour plate over their direct vision laminated ballistic glass blocks. They could then flip down their overhead fixed periscope as seen here and continue to operate the vehicle. As with all tanks, it normally falls to the vehicle commander to tell the driver what to do as their visibility is so limited. (*David Marian*)

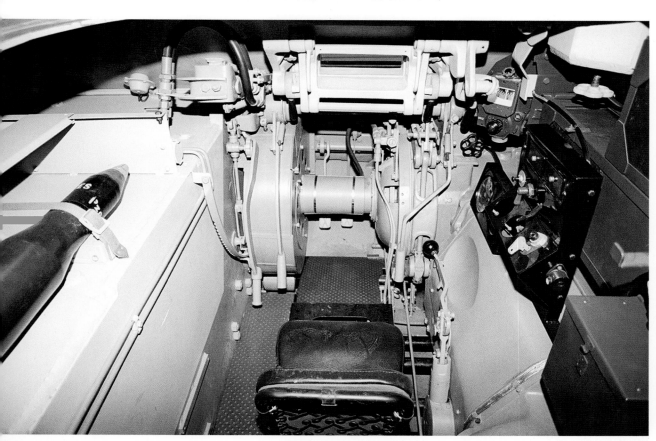

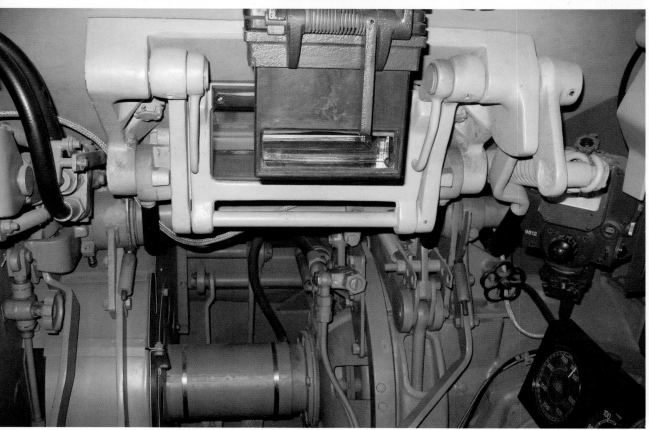

(**Above**) Pictured is an unrestored Panther Ausf. A. With the introduction of the new spherical cast-armoured mount armed with a machine gun and fitted with an optical sight in the glacis of the Ausf. A, the radioman's forward-facing periscope was deleted as seen here. Early-production Ausf. A tanks retained a pistol port on the right-hand side of the turret, which is missing here. (*Ian Wilcox*)

(**Opposite, above**) Seen here in the hull of a Panther Ausf. A undergoing restoration is an incomplete turret basket. The gunner's seat is on the left and the loader's fold-up seat on the right. Both are missing their normal seat cushions. In-between them is the light-grey painted compressor that provided the air for the main gun bore evacuator. Also visible is the very large spent cartridge case bin. (*Author's collection*)

(**Opposite, below**) A side view of the lower turret basket of a Panther Ausf. A. Note the wire mesh, which was intended to make sure that the ejected main gun cartridge cases dropped into the spent cartridge case bin rather than onto the floor of the turret basket. When fired, the Panther's main gun recoiled almost 17-inches rearward into the turret. (*English translation by James D. Brown*)

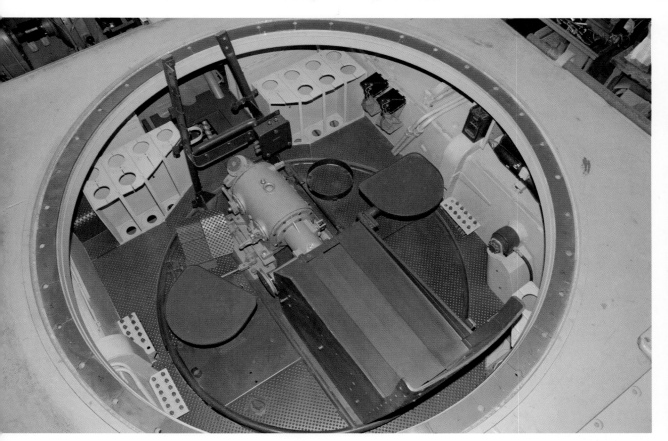

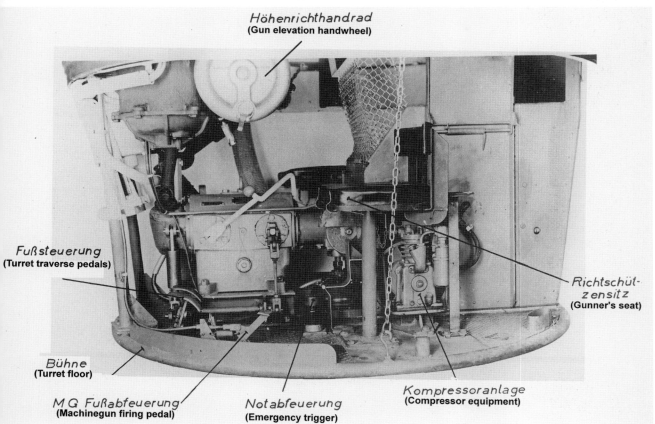

Höhenrichthandrad
(Gun elevation handwheel)

Fußsteuerung
(Turret traverse pedals)

Richtschützensitz
(Gunner's seat)

Bühne
(Turret floor)

MG Fußabfeuerung
(Machinegun firing pedal)

Notabfeuerung
(Emergency trigger)

Kompressoranlage
(Compressor equipment)

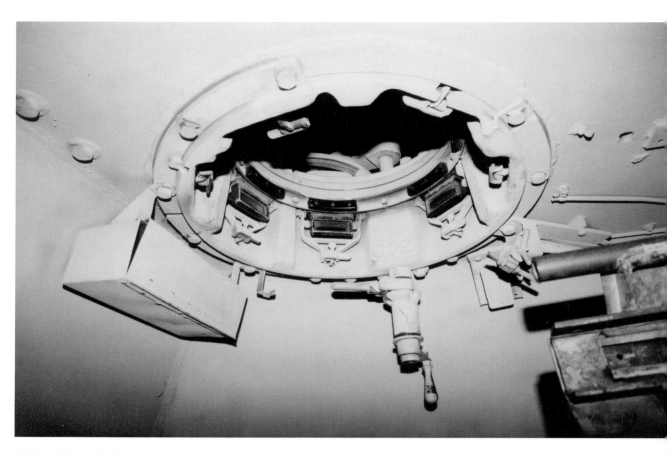

(**Opposite, above**) Looking upwards from the bottom of a Panther tank turret floor is the cast-armour vehicle commander's cupola. It first appeared on the Panther Ausf. A and remained on the succeeding model. The vertically-oriented object protruding downward from the cupola is the hand crank for the vehicle commander to open and close his overhead hatch. (*Author's collection*)

(**Opposite, below**) The reason for the eventual elimination of the right-hand side turret pistol port on the Panther Ausf. A was the fitting of a breech-loading anti-personnel grenade-launcher seen here. It was known in German as the *Nahverteidigungswaffe* (close defence weapon). It was mounted in the turret roof over the loader's position. It could be traversed 360 degrees and also fire smoke grenades. (*Author's collection*)

(**Above**) A design feature of the Panther Ausf. A that was not seen on the Panther Ausf. D turret was a fixed forward-looking periscope on the right-hand side of the turret roof for the loader. In this picture we see the loader's view of that replaceable periscope in its frame holder. This design feature would be retained for the next model in the Panther tank series. (*Chun-lun Hsu*)

(**Above**) Note the binocular gun sight apertures on this restored Panther Ausf. A despite it being fitted with a monocular gun sight. In such cases one of the two openings in the gun shield was plugged. This would continue until such time that new gun shields with only one aperture in the gun shield starting showing up on the Panther Ausf. A assembly lines. (*Chris Hughes*)

(**Opposite, above**) Starting in January 1944, all new-production Panther Ausf. A tanks left the factory floor with an arrangement of three pipes on the left side of the rear hull plate as seen here on this preserved Ausf. A. The centre pipe remained an engine exhaust pipe, with those on either side being added to improve engine-cooling. On the right-hand side of the rear hull plate remained a single engine exhaust pipe. (*David T. Lin*)

(**Opposite, below**) All the powertrain and related components of the Panther tank are shown in this illustration. It was the requirement for the floor of the turret basket to clear the drive shaft that ran from the engine to the front hull mounted transmission, which helped dictate the height of the Panther tank turret as it had with previous German-designed and built tanks. (*English translation by James D. Brown*)

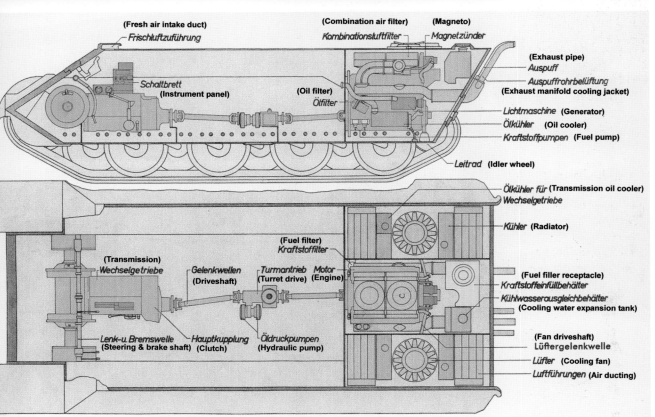

(Fresh air intake duct)
Frischluftzuführung

(Combination air filter)
Kombinationsluftfilter

(Magneto)
Magnetzünder

Schaltbrett
(Instrument panel)

(Oil filter)
Ölfilter

(Exhaust pipe)
Auspuff
Auspuffrohrbelüftung
(Exhaust manifold cooling jacket)

Lichtmaschine **(Generator)**
Ölkühler **(Oil cooler)**
Kraftstoffpumpen **(Fuel pump)**

Leitrad **(Idler wheel)**

Ölkühler für **(Transmission oil cooler)**
Wechselgetriebe

Kühler **(Radiator)**

(Transmission)
Wechselgetriebe

Gelenkwellen
(Driveshaft)

Turmantrieb
(Turret drive)

Motor
(Engine)

(Fuel filter)
Kraftstofffilter

(Fuel filler receptacle)
Kraftstoffeinfüllbehälter

Kühlwasserausgleichbehälter
(Cooling water expansion tank)

(Fan driveshaft)
Lüftergelenkwelle

Lüfter **(Cooling fan)**
Luftführungen **(Air ducting)**

Lenk-u. Bremswelle
(Steering & brake shaft)

Hauptkupplung
(Clutch)

Öldruckpumpen
(Hydraulic pump)

(**Opposite, above**) The Panther tank rear hull was divided into three compartments as seen here. The engine was located in the centre. Up until August 1943, the engine compartment was designed to be watertight. This was done so that the vehicle could ford deep-water obstacles when bridges of suitable carrying capacity were not available. (*Patton Museum*)

(**Above**) Pictured is a rebuilt example of a second-generation Panther tank engine designated the Maybach HL230 P30. It generated 700hp at 3,000rpm and began appearing on Panther Ausf. D tanks coming off the assembly lines in May 1943. The first-generation version of the engine was considered underpowered as it generated only 650hp at 3,000rpm. (*David Marian*)

(**Opposite, below**) With the spaced armour-plating on either side of this restored Panther Ausf. A the tank had a width of 11ft 3in. Because of the haste with which the Panther tank series was placed into production, there would be an almost endless number of small internal and external design modifications. The various model designations for the Panther tank series reflect only the most major design changes. (*Author's collection*)

(**Opposite, above**) Two knocked-out Panther Ausf. A tanks in Normandy, France. The Ausf. A was fitted with a two-speed hydraulic power turret traverse system. The turret could be rotated 360 degrees in just fifteen seconds with the engine at maximum rpm. When the Ausf. A engine was later de-rated it added an extra three seconds for the vehicle's turret to be rotated 360 degrees. (*Patton Museum*)

(**Opposite, below**) On display at a US army museum is this unrestored Panther Ausf. A. As with the Panther Ausf. D, the superstructure side plates on the Ausf. A consisted of two armour plates, both 40mm thick. The larger of the two was sloped at 40 degrees. The smaller wedge-shaped superstructure plate had no slope and was welded to the bottom rear of the main superstructure side plate. (*Christophe Vallier*)

(**Above**) The main spotting feature of the Panther Ausf. G was a large sloped single-piece superstructure plate on either side of the vehicle. That design feature is clearly seen here on a turretless Panther Ausf. G hull being restored at a French museum. Note the horizontal bar running across a portion of the superstructure. This was for the attachment of lower hull spaced armour plates. (*David T. Lin*)

In this illustration of a Panther Ausf. G from various angles we see the driver's new 360-degree rotating and tilting periscope. Also visible is the loader's fixed overhead periscope that had first appeared on the Panther Ausf. A turret. Behind the radioman's turret roof-mounted periscope is the small opening for the *Nahverteidigungswaffe*. (*George Bradford*)

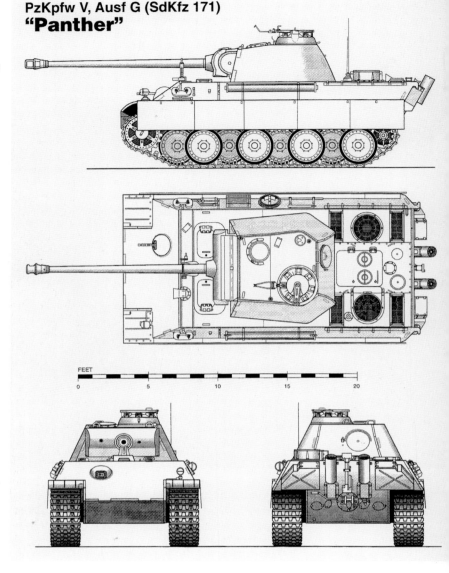

PzKpfw V, Ausf G (SdKfz 171)
"Panther"

FEET
0   5   10   15   20

(**Opposite, above**) A secondary design spotting feature for the Panther Ausf. G, which can be seen here on a restored and running example, was the deletion of the driver's glacis-mounted direct vision port. In its place the driver on the Panther Ausf. G was provided with an overhead tilting periscope sight that could be rotated 360 degrees. (*Andreas Kirchhoff*)

(**Opposite, below**) On display as a monument tank in Western Europe is this unrestored Panther Ausf. G. Missing from this vehicle's barrel is the main gun muzzle brake. Harder-to-spot design identifying features of the Ausf. G were new simplified overhead armour hatches for the driver and radioman. The external tool storage arrangement on the Ausf. G also changed. (*Ian Wilcox*)

Visible in this picture of a restored Panther Ausf. G is the driver's 360-degree rotating and tilting periscope. On the previous Panther Ausf. D and Ausf. A the driver had two overhead fixed periscopes, one pointing directly forward and the other angled off to the right-hand side. Behind the driver's periscope is the tank's main gun barrel travel lock. *(Andreas Kirchhoff)*

(**Opposite, above**) A knocked-out Panther Ausf. G. With this model of the Panther tank series the roof of the turret was fitted with three small welded-on fixtures to provide anchor points for the mounting of a portable 4,409lb jib boom for lifting out the vehicle's front hull-mounted transmission. In addition, the Ausf. G had longer steel tow cables, which are seen in this photograph. *(Patton Museum)*

(**Opposite, below**) Belonging to a British museum is this Panther Ausf. G. The gun tube on all German tanks is referred to as the *Rohr*. In the case of the Panther tank series the gun tube/barrel was a one-piece steel forging weighing approximately 2,400lb. The double-baffle muzzle brake at the end of the barrel was to help reduce recoil and weighed 69lb. *(Tank Museum)*

This line illustration shows the main gun ammunition storage arrangement in the lower hull/superstructure of the Panther Ausf. G. Missing from this drawing are the three main gun rounds stored under the tank's turret basket. Whereas the Panther Ausf. D and Ausf. A had authorized storage for seventy-nine main gun rounds, the Ausf. G had authorized storage for eighty-two main gun rounds. (*Tank Museum*)

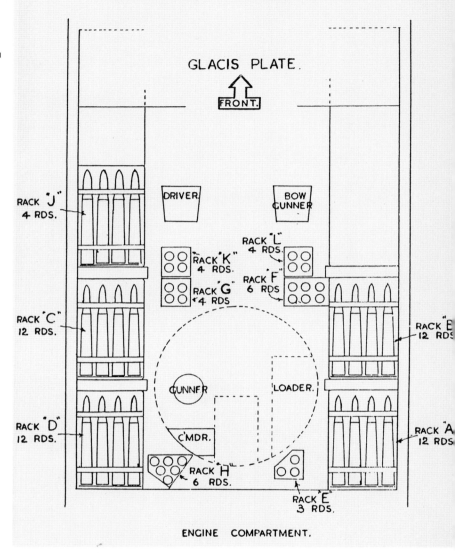

'PANTHER'

PLAN OF AMMUNITION STOWAGE.

(**Opposite, above**) Appearing on some examples of the Panther Ausf. G was the slightly revised machine-gun-equipped ball mount seen here. It had a stepped lower embrasure intended to reduce the amount of bullet splash entering the ball mount. The machine gun mounted in the Panther tank series was the well-known 7.92mm M34. The tank-mounted version was designated the M34T. (*Martin Morgan*)

(**Opposite, below**) Not seen on previous models of the Panther tank series was this raised fighting compartment heater known in German as the *Kampfraumheizung* seen here on the rear engine deck of an unrestored Panther Ausf. G. This design feature started showing up on the Ausf. G production lines in October 1944. (*Chun-Iun Hsu*)

(**Opposite, above**) On this unrestored Panther Ausf. G we see two square welded armoured boxes around the bottom of the two engine exhaust manifold pipes. This design feature began appearing on the Ausf. G assembly lines in May 1944. On previous models of the tank they were rounded and made of cast armour. The sheet metal covers over the engine exhaust manifold pipes began appearing on the Ausf. G beginning in June 1944. (*Christophe Vallier*)

(**Above**) Beginning in October 1944, the stop-gap measure of hiding the glow from the two engine exhaust manifold pipes on the Panther Ausf. G with sheet metal covers was discontinued. In its place they were covered with a lightweight rubberized housing referred to by the Germans as the *Flammenvernichter* (flame suppressor) and seen here on a restored Panther Ausf. G. (*David Marian*)

(**Opposite, below**) Visible in this picture of a restored Panther Ausf. G turret we can see the sheet metal debris guard over the gap behind the gun shield that began appearing on the Ausf. G production lines in August 1944. The aperture for the M34T 7.92mm machine gun is also visible in this picture, as is the armoured hood for the loader's fixed periscope (missing here). (*Andreas Kirchhoff*)

Two design features of the Panther Ausf. G appear in this photograph. First is the lengthened rain guard over the gunner's sight aperture that began showing up on the Ausf. G production line in September 1944. The second is the addition of the chin on the lower portion of the gun shield, which also began appearing on the Ausf. G assembly lines in September 1944. (*Patton Museum*)

From a British army wartime report comes this line illustration of the various dimensions of the new chin gun shield for the Panther Ausf. G. That being said, the implementation of such design changes on any of the Second World War German-designed and built tanks typically occurred gradually over varying lengths of time. (*Tank Museum*)

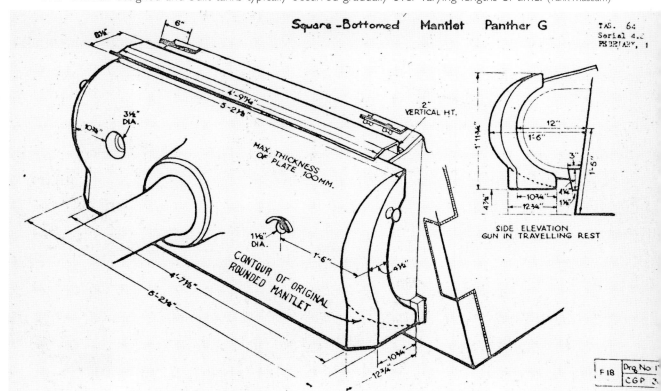

On display at a US army museum is this unrestored Panther Ausf. A with the chin gun shield. Other changes made to the Ausf. G during its production run included the elimination of two of the vehicle's four shock absorbers/shock dampers in October 1944. In the same month, provisions were made to allow the driver to operate his vehicle with his overhead hatch opened. (*Christophe Vallier*)

A column of British army vehicles is shown passing a knocked-out/abandoned Panther Ausf. G with the chin turret gun shield. Note the addition of spare track links to the turret side of the vehicle. This arrangement shows up in many images of late-war Panther tanks and no doubt reflected the concerns of the crew about flank shots to the thinner armour sides of the Panther tank turret. (*Tank Museum*)

(**Above**) To correct all the design shortcomings of the Panther tank series turrets uncovered in combat, German industry began work on a much-redesigned turret for the Panther Ausf. F, the planned replacement on the assembly lines for the Panther Ausf. G. The new experimental turret for the proposed Panther Ausf. F that never made it into production is seen here. (*Tank Museum*)

(**Opposite, above**) Pictured is the Type 3 *Chi-Hu* medium tank armed with a high-velocity 75mm main gun. This gun was intended as an anti-tank weapon, whereas the low-velocity version mounted in the Type 2 *Chi-Hu* medium tank was optimized for firing high-explosive (HE) rounds used against enemy infantry and defensive positions. Note the muzzle brake that had not been seen on any previous Japanese tank. (*Patton Museum*)

(**Opposite, below**) Pictured during the American early post-war occupation of Japan is an American soldier posing on a Type 4 *Chi-To* medium tank. It was armed with a high-velocity 75mm main gun optimized for the anti-tank role. The first completed example of the tank rolled off the production line just before the Japanese surrender and therefore none ever saw combat. (*Patton Museum*)

Chapter Four

Heavy Tanks

Almost the entire story of Axis heavy tanks in the Second World War can be summed up in a single tank series: the German Tiger tanks. Only German industry possessed the industrial capability to design and build a heavy tank weighing over 100,000lb among the various Axis nations. Even then, their construction would impose a heavy burden on the already badly-strained military-industrial complex.

The German army had not envisioned a requirement for a heavy tank prior to their summer invasion of France in 1940. It was the belated discovery of the firepower and armour protection inferiority of their medium tanks compared to some of the French and British army tanks encountered that had prompted Adolf Hitler to suggest that a new heavily-armed and armoured heavy tank was the solution.

Getting it Built

The German army Ordnance Department was not in favour of heavy tanks because of the tactical problems inherent with road, rail and bridge weight restrictions within Europe at that time. To placate Hitler, the weapon design office of the Ordnance Department commissioned automotive engineer Dr Ferdinand Porsche to design a heavy tank chassis in the autumn of 1940.

In a May 1941 meeting, Hitler, having lost his patience with the German army Ordnance Department's lack of progress in fielding a heavy tank, took personal charge of the project. He awarded Porsche and the firm of Henschel & Son contracts for the chassis for six prototype heavy tanks each, to be ready for his inspection on 20 April 1942 (his birthday). Krupp was assigned the job of designing and building the turrets for both contenders' vehicles.

Choices

By late 1940, both Porsche and Henschel had acquired the engineering talent to produce a heavy tank design that would meet Hitler's requirements. Dr Porsche was so convinced that he would win the competition over Henschel owing to his superior product and his close friendship with the German leader that he started production without a contract.

Porsche therefore went ahead and contracted with Krupp to build 100 chassis to his design specifications and 100 Krupp-designed turrets. The new tank was designated the VK 45.01(P) and would weigh approximately 100,000lb.

Henschel, which had been working on a heavy tank weighing less than 40 tons, was blind-sided by the new 100,000lb requirement. It forced them to cobble together available components in order to meet Hitler's birthday deadline. Henschel's new prototype heavy tank chassis was assigned the designation VK 45.01(H).

Unfortunately, while Hitler had favoured the mounting of a Rheinmetall-Borsig AG-designed and built 88mm gun on whichever heavy tank was chosen, the already-selected Krupp turret to be mounted on both contender submissions was incapable of being fitted with the large and heavy Rheinmetall-Borsig AG gun. The compromise was a smaller and lighter Krupp-designed and built 88mm gun designated the 8.8cm KwK 36 L/56.

The Famous Name Appears

The Porsche and Henschel chassis fell under a procurement project referred to as the *Tiger-Programm*. The vehicle then went through a number of designation changes during its rapid development period. The first 'Tiger tank' reference occurred in February 1942 when it appeared in German military documents as the 'Tiger H1'. The following month it appeared as the Panzer VI (VK 45.01(H)) Ausf. H1 (Tiger).

On 20 April 1942, Porsche and Henschel presented their respective Tiger tank chassis for Hitler's inspection. While neither vehicle was quite ready for production, it was clear that the Henschel prototype was superior. After the showing, Hitler turned to Albert Speer (his civilian minister of armament) to arrange for continued testing of the two prototype Tiger tank chassis to see which best met the German army's requirements.

This summary of the decision-making process for picking a winning contender between the Porsche and Henschel candidate Tiger tank chassis appears in an extract from a book titled *Tiger: The History of a Legendary Weapon 1942–1945* by Egon Kleine and Volkmar Kühn:

> The most important military demand of the new tank was that the vehicle should be available in large numbers by the beginning of summer 1943 at the latest. Following extensive testing the Henschel Tiger was unanimously chosen as the superior of the two tanks. The electric drive of the Porsche Tiger was highly interesting, but it was much too complicated to be serviced with the simple means available to the front-line units, especially in the Russian theatre.

Production Commences

Most of the 100 chassis that Krupp built for Porsche's rejected heavy tank design later appeared as tank destroyers armed with a casemated Krupp-designed and built

88mm main gun designated the 8.8cm PaK 43/2 L/71. The Krupp-designed and built turrets ordered by Porsche went through a modification process to fit them to the Henschel production chassis.

The first Tiger tank rolled off the Henschel production line in August 1942. The production designation became Panzer VI Ausf. E in early March 1943. Hereafter, the designation 'Tiger E' will be employed throughout the remainder of the work for the sake of brevity. At the same time, the unofficial name 'Tiger I' tank came into use, which is the name most often used even today. The Western Allies tended to refer to the vehicle as the 'Mark VI' in their written reports. The ordnance inventory number was 181.

Description

On 16 January 1943, the Red Army captured an intact Tiger E and subjected it to extensive testing to uncover any weak points they could exploit in battle. The British army captured its first intact Tiger E on 21 April 1943 in North Africa. That vehicle survived the war years and has resided in the collection of the Tank Museum located in Bovington, England ever since.

In their investigation of the captured Tiger E the British army discovered that the tank's weight was approximately 112,000lbs, a big jump compared to the approximately 100,000lb design limit the Germans themselves had set for the vehicle. That weight gain no doubt reflected the continued emphasis by Hitler and the German army on providing the tank with enough armour protection to survive any tanks or armoured fighting vehicles the Red Army then had in service and might field in the near future.

After a close study of the captured Tiger E, a number of detailed reports on the tank's design and construction were passed on to the US army. A passage from one of those original reports describes the most noticeable external features of the vehicle:

As compared with other AFVs in service [late 1943], the Tiger is outstandingly well armed and protected. Designed to carry an 8.8 cm gun and constructed of very heavy armour plate, the vehicle is naturally of exceptional size and weight and it is therefore somewhat surprising to note how it is, to a certain degree, dwarfed by the main armament. Viewed from the side with the turret at 12 o'clock, the 8.8cm gun extends beyond the nose of the tank by about a quarter of its length, and the length from the muzzle brake to the mantlet [gun shield] is rather over half the total length of the vehicle.

The British army measured their first captured Tiger E's hull as 20ft 8.5in long. The front overhang of the main gun increased the length to 27ft 9in. The overall width of the vehicle, including the mudguards, was 12ft 3in and the height was 9ft 4.5in.

Firepower

According to results of gunnery tests conducted by the British army on a captured Tiger E, the accuracy of the main gun was excellent. The test showed:

A five-round grouping 16 × 18 [inches] was obtained at 1,200 yards. Five rounds were fired at targets moving at 15mph and, although smoke obscured observation by the gunner, three hits were scored after directions were given by the commander. Normal rate of fire was estimated to be from five to eight rounds per minute.

At a range of 2,187 yards the Tiger E's standard APCBC-HE projectile could penetrate 83mm of armour. A wartime German army document stated that Tiger E crews had no problem in achieving first-round hits on Red Army T-34 medium tanks at ranges anywhere between 656 and 1,093 yards. The APCBC-HE projectiles fired from the Tiger E's main gun often passed through the front of the T-34 tank's hull armour and still possessed enough velocity to continue through the vehicle and destroy its engine in the rear hull.

Armour Protection

The near-vertical glacis of the Tiger E was 102mm thick with the front hull plate directly below and in front of it being sloped at 80 degrees and 61mm thick. The lower front hull nose plate was 102mm thick and sloped at 24 degrees. The horseshoe-shaped turret was 82mm thick with a turret roof that was originally 26mm thick and eventually brought up to approximately 50mm. The large vertical gun shield was up to 205mm thick with the armour behind it 100mm thick.

In a report appears this short extract by a young German officer on the damage to his Tiger E suffered in early February 1943 while doing battle with the Red Army:

We counted 227 hits from anti-tank rifle rounds [14.5mm], 14 hits from 5.7cm [57mm] and 4.5cm [45mm] anti-tank guns, and 11 hits from 7.62cm [76.2mm] guns. The right track and suspension were heavily damaged. Several road wheels and their suspension arms were perforated. The idler wheel had worked out of its mount. In spite of all this damage, the Tiger still managed to cover an additional 60 kilometres under its own power.

The armour plates on the Tiger E hull and turret were joined together by overlapping stepped welded joints dovetailed together for both mechanical strength and armour performance. The only exceptions to that were the cast-armour gun shield and the later version vehicle commander's cupola.

Tank Commander

In battle, a Tiger E tank commander controlled the movement and fire of his vehicle. His effectiveness in battle depended on how well he and his crew worked together.

When a target appeared, the tank commander decided whether or not to engage it. The commander also decided which weapon to use and the type of ammunition that would most effectively destroy the target.

Unlike the Panzer III and IV medium tanks in which the tank commander was located directly behind the breech of the main gun, on the Tiger E the tank commander's position was on the left-hand side of the vehicle's main gun recoil guard, with the gunner directly in front and below him. This was the same arrangement as on the Panther medium tank series.

On the early production units of the Tiger E there had been a pressed sheet metal guard plate bolted to the roof of the turret on the commander's right-hand side. It was intended to protect his right elbow when the main gun went into recoil. It was later replaced with a fireproof cloth flap to improve the ability of the tank commander to communicate with the loader.

Gunner

The job of a gunner on any Second World War tank, including the Tiger E, was to fire and adjust the main gun and coaxial machine gun under the direction of the tank commander. While observation from his position was always limited on all tanks, he often did assist the tank commander in acquiring targets. A British army report describes the Tiger E tank gunner's position in detail:

> The gunner sits in front of the [tank] commander on the left side of the main armament. His seat is elliptically shaped and padded. It is mounted on a horizontal arm and is not adjustable. The backrest is also padded and curved to fit the gunner's back. Although the seat and backrest are comfortable, the position is very cramped. The gunner's feet rest, with toes pointing downwards, on the power traverse footplate, which is centred only eight inches in front of and 12 inches below the seat.

The Tiger E's main gun was fired electrically by the gunner with a curved steel bar pivoted on the shaft of the main gun manually-operating elevation wheel. The bar could be operated with one finger by the gunner. The coaxial machine gun was operated by the gunner's right foot. Besides his optical sighting instruments, the only other exterior vision for the Tiger E gunner was a vision slit in the turret wall to his left, protected by thick laminated ballistic glass.

Loader

The Tiger E loader was located on the right side of the main gun. The breech of the weapon and the recoil guard divided the turret into two separate half-sections. The loader was also responsible for the loading and servicing of the coaxial machine gun mounted on his side of the turret. The loader in all German tanks was considered the lowest-ranking man among the crew.

The Tiger E loader had an overhead hatch but could also leave the vehicle by means of a circular escape hatch in the right rear quarter of the turret wall. A wartime Tiger E tank battalion report describes the various uses of the rear turret escape hatch on the vehicle:

> The hatch is not only there for egress when in great danger, but also for the evacuation of the wounded, for establishing contact with nearby infantry, for tossing out spent cartridge cases, and for extinguishing engine compartment fires in battle from the hatch by traversing the turret to the 3 o'clock position. It is also used for egress to conduct the work needed for towing disabled tanks in battle.

A turret basket underneath the Tiger E turret attached to the turret ring with three pillars. All three crewmen in the vehicle's turret had seats attached to the turret ring, although the loader had to stand on the turret basket floorboard in order to load the main gun and to load and service the coaxial machine gun.

Driver

In battle, tank drivers are continuously looking for firing positions that also afford protection from enemy observation and fire. They must always be prepared to bring the vehicle to a gradual halt to allow firing of the main gun. The driver must also smoothly drive the tank when the vehicle's machine guns were in use against stationary targets. In his memoirs, Otto Carius describes the importance of the driver:

> Obviously, the greatest responsibility for the readiness of the vehicle fell to the driver. The man really had to be top notch. He had to drive using his head and not his 'rear end'. If he was on his toes, then his 'Tiger' never left him in the lurch. The really good tank driver – and no other type was let loose on a 'Tiger' – also had to have an instinctive feel for the terrain.

In addition to the driver's visor, early versions of the Tiger E included a binocular periscope directly above the driver's visor in the glacis. Their 65-degree field of view allowed the driver to operate the vehicle with the visor closed. The binocular periscope disappeared from production vehicles beginning in February 1943. Those hulls that showed up with the two openings for the binocular periscope still drilled out had welded plugs inserted in their place.

In many tank designs, the driver's overhead hatch is directly above his seat, so he may operate the vehicle 'opened up' with his head and upper torso projecting out over the superstructure roof. As already mentioned, the designers of the Tiger E did not see that as necessary and made no provision for it and, in fact, the driver's overhead hatch on the Tiger E, as well as the radioman's overhead hatch, were offset a bit to either side of the tank's front superstructure.

Radioman

The radioman sat in the right front corner of the Tiger E superstructure and had an overhead circular armoured hatch, 19in in diameter, as did the driver. Both hatches hinged at the outside edge and were spring-balanced, with a catch to lock them in a half-opened position. Unlike the driver's seat, the radioman's seat was not adjustable.

The amplitude modulated (AM) voice radio in the standard Tiger E sat on top of the transmission housing that divided the radioman's position from the driver's position. Platoon leaders or company headquarters tanks had an extra radio that was also mounted on top of the tank's transmission housing.

A New Tiger Tank Appears

As early as May 1942, a month after the first Tiger E prototypes appeared, a decision was made to start the development of the next generation heavy tank. This came about because it was clear that future Red Army tank and anti-tank gun development would eventually render the German army's existing tank inventory obsolete.

As with the Tiger E, the final contenders for the chassis of this proposed next-generation heavy tank were Porsche and Henschel. The winning chassis was to be fitted with a Krupp-designed and built turret armed with a Krupp-designed and built 88mm gun designated the 8.8cm KwK 43 L/71. This was despite Hitler and the German army preferring a more powerful 88mm Rheinmetall-Borsig AG gun, which proved too large to fit in the Krupp-designed turret.

As with the Tiger E competition, the overconfident Dr Ferdinand Porsche once again began ordering components for his next generation before a contract was awarded. This included fifty Krupp-built turrets based on his design. However, much to Porsche's dismay, the Henschel chassis proved to be the superior product and won the competition.

The Winner

The Henschel-designed next-generation heavy tank chassis fitted with a Krupp-built turret armed with a Krupp main gun would go on to become the Panzer VI Ausf. B, hereafter referred to as the 'Tiger B'. It was assigned the ordnance inventory number 182. The American and British armies referred to it as the 'Tiger II', or the occasionally-used German name *Königstiger* (King Tiger or Royal Tiger).

The fifty Porsche-designed turrets built by Krupp were modified and fitted to the first fifty production units of the Tiger B chassis. Thereafter, all the Henschel-produced Tiger B chassis units were fitted with a Krupp-designed and built turret referred to as the *Serienturm* (production series turret).

Production

Pre-production of the Tiger B at Henschel's plant started in December 1943 with three evaluation vehicles fitted with the Porsche turrets. Early-production units of the

Tiger began coming off the assembly lines in January 1944 with all being assigned to training units between February and May 1944. The tank was not issued to combat units until June 1944.

Of the 1,500 units of the Tiger B ordered by the German army, only 489 made it into service before the war in Europe ended. German mismanagement of the Tiger B programme, Western Allied air bombardment of German factories involved in building the Tiger B and the country's transportation infrastructure contributed to the very low numbers built.

Description

A British army report listed the Tiger B as being 23ft 10in long excluding the main gun and 32ft 8in long with the main gun pointed directly over the front of the hull. With the mudflaps fitted, the Tiger B was 11ft 11in wide. The tank was 10ft 2in high. Reflecting the size increase over the Tiger E and its thicker armour protection, the Tiger B weighed approximately 150,000lb.

As with the capture of all new enemy weapons, both the Axis and the Allies were quick to evaluate them and issue reports to identify design trends as well as to sometimes point out weak points in their respective designs that could be taken advantage of on the battlefield. In a US army technical report dated 13 September 1944, information on the Tiger B layout and armament appears:

> A badly-damaged specimen of the new redesigned Tiger tank, mounting the 8.8cm KwK 43 L/71 gun, Sd.Kfz.182, has been examined in the British sector in Normandy. This tank bears little resemblance to the previous Tiger tank [E], first encountered in North Africa, but has many features in common with the Panther, particularly as regards the sloping of the main armour plates. However, it would be a mistake to compare it with any previous German tank, as it mounts a gun with a much superior performance to the gun in either the previous Tiger [E] or Panther tanks and its armour affords a much greater degree of protection.

Firepower

As with the Tiger E, the Tiger B's main gun was provided with an HE round to deal with non-armoured targets. The standard AP projectile fired by the main gun on the Tiger B was able to deal with any Allied tanks encountered on the battlefields of 1944 as appears in this passage from a September 1944 US army report:

> The standard full-bore AP round for the Tiger B tank's 8.8cm gun was an APCBC round known as the Pzgr.39/43, whose muzzle velocity of 3,340 feet per second gave exceptional armour penetration performance. At a range of 500 yards, it could penetrate more than 7 inches [175mm] of steel armour, 6.5 inches [163mm] at 1,000 yards, and 5 inches [125mm] at 1 mile.

In a German army wartime document it was reported that the main gun on the Tiger B easily destroyed the latest Red Army heavy tank known as the 'Stalin' at ranges of up to 1,640 yards. The Red Army T-34 medium tanks were dealt with at ranges of up to 3,280 yards. Such was the fear of the combat effectiveness of the Tiger B's main gun that the same report claimed the crews of Red Army tanks and self-propelled guns often retreated upon losing their first vehicle to a Tiger B.

Those Tiger B tanks with the Porsche turrets had authorized storage for eighty main gun rounds. When fitted with the production series turret the tank had authorized storage for eighty-six main gun rounds. The majority of main gun rounds for the Tiger B were stored in the hull, with a smaller number stored in the turret bustle of the tank. There are wartime reports that some Tiger B crews refused to store main gun rounds in the turret bustle as they felt it was safer to keep them all in the hull.

Protection

The front of the production series turret for the Tiger B was 180mm thick and sloped at 9 degrees. The front of the Porsche turret was rounded and ranged in thickness from 60mm to 100mm. The sides and rear turret walls of both types of Tiger B turrets were 80mm thick with different degrees of sloping. The roof of the production series turret was 44mm thick with a maximum 10-degree slope and that of the Porsche turret 40mm thick with a maximum slope of 12 degrees.

The Tiger B glacis was sloped at 50 degrees and the armour was 150mm thick. The lower front hull plate was sloped at 50 degrees and was 100mm thick. The superstructure sides were sloped at 25 degrees and were 80mm thick. The vertical hull sides before the Tiger B superstructure were 80mm thick. The rear hull plate was sloped at 30 degrees and was 80mm thick. The superstructure roof was 40mm thick.

Crew Positions

Like the gunner on the Tiger E, the Tiger B gunner fired the main gun electrically. The trigger for the main gun consisted of a steel bar hinged to the shaft cover of the elevating wheel, located next to the gunner's right hand, the bar being curved and lying parallel to the rim of the elevating wheel.

A British army report describes the Tiger B driver's position:

> Since the [driver's] seat is adjustable for upper and lower positions, the controls have been designed to be accessible when the driver is in either position. Power-assisted steering is controlled by a semi-circular wheel one foot three inches in diameter. The wheel column is jointed and the wheel can be raised or lowered to suit the driver's position.

The Tiger B driver could drive 'opened-up' with his head and upper torso projecting out over the superstructure roof. By contrast, Tiger E drivers could only drive 'closed down'. As with the Tiger E, the designers of the Tiger B provided the turret crew with an escape hatch in the rear of the vehicle's turret. British army tests of this hatch (which opened outward and downwards) led them to believe that it was of dubious value due to its small size and the main gun rounds that might be stored there.

Design Strong Points

A good tank design is a balance of firepower, protection, mobility and reliability. Firepower and protection of both Tiger variants is legendary. With regard to firepower, the long-range main guns of both Tiger tanks and their superior fire-control systems for their day provided them with an impressive kill ratio, and according to author Christopher W. Wilbeck in his book *Sledgehammers: Strengths and Flaws of Tiger Tank Battalions in World War II*: 'Whatever mission heavy tank battalions were given, their primary task was to destroy enemy tanks. In so doing, they were undeniably successful. The kill ratio of heavy tank battalions when measured against Tigers lost in direct combat is an impressive 12.2 to 1.'

In a book titled *T-34 in Action* edited by Artem Drabkin and Oleg Sheremet there is a quote by a Red Army tanker describing the firepower advantage German Tiger tanks had on the battlefields of the Eastern Front when in open country:

> Just try to approach them, they'd burn your tank from 1,200 to 1,500 metres! They were cocky! In essence, until we got our 85mm guns we had to run from Tigers like rabbits and look for an opportunity to turn back and get at their flanks. It was difficult. If you saw a Tiger at 800 to 1,000 metres crossing you while it moved its gun horizontally you could stay in your tank. But once it started moving vertically, you'd better jump out or you'd get burned. It never happened to me, but other guys bailed out.

An important aspect of the Tiger tank success on the battlefield was its optical sighting systems. Beginning in April 1944, the Tiger B was fitted with an articulated monocular telescopic sight similar to the one that was fitted to the Tiger E beginning in March 1944. Prior to being fitted with an articulated monocular telescopic sight, both Tiger tanks had been fitted with articulated binocular sights.

US army Sergeant Lewis A. Taylor of the 2nd Armored Division had this to say about the German optical tank sights in a March 1945 report: 'The German telescopic sights mounted in their tanks are far superior to ours. In particular, it is more powerful. In fact all their optical equipment is superior to ours.'

Design Weak Spots

In spite of their firepower and armour protection advantages, the mobility and reliability of the Tiger tanks constituted their weaker aspects. Reliability usually includes not only robustness of the mechanical design but also ease of repair or replacement of components. The Achilles' heel of the Tigers was their powertrain, which caused more to be lost to mechanical failure than to combat damage.

In both versions of the Tiger tanks, the 2,860lb Maybach liquid-cooled, gasoline-powered aircraft-type engine was centrally located at the rear of the hull. Large radiators sat on either side of the engine compartment. Engine torque in the Tiger tanks was transmitted to the transmission located in-between the driver and radio-man in the front hull.

Engine Details

The first 250 production Tiger Es had Maybach V-12 1,302 cubic inch engines, designated HL210 P45, rated at 650hp at 3,000rpm. However, frequent engine failures in service resulted in the governed speed being lowered to 2,500rpm. The result was that the Tiger E found itself to be considered underpowered by many.

The HL210 engine was upgraded to 700hp and re-designated the HL230 P45, starting in May 1943. The Germans replaced the original aluminium cylinder block with a cast-iron cylinder block, which allowed them to increase the displacement by almost 12 per cent to 1,457 cubic inches. This engine powered late-production Tiger E and HL230 variants powered the Tiger B.

However, like its predecessor, the HL230 engine lacked the durability to run for long periods at rated speed. To prolong engine service life, the builders had the engine de-rated to 650hp in November 1943 by reducing the governed speed to 2,500rpm, making the heavier Tiger B even more underpowered than the Tiger E.

Transmissions

The Tiger E featured a Maybach-designed hydraulically-operated semi-automatic transmission designated Olvar 40 12 16. The Tiger B was equipped with an upgraded version designated Olvar 40 12 16 *Ausführung* B (model B). Both versions provided eight forward and four reverse gear ratios.

Mechanical power from the rear-mounted Tiger E and Tiger B engines travelled to the transmission through a driveshaft that ran underneath the turret basket floor. The gearshift lever in both versions of the Tiger tanks was located to the driver's right and mounted on the side of the transmission housing that was located between the driver and radioman positions.

Tiger tank transmissions were semi-automatic. This meant that the drivers were not required to use the clutch to manually disengage the drive train for every gear change. Clutching was only required to start the vehicle and to switch between forward and reverse. Hydraulically-activated clutches in the transmission eliminated the need for manual clutching by the driver.

Steering Gear and Suspension Systems

Due to the weight of the Tiger E, the German firm of Henschel decided to adopt a double-differential steering system for the vehicle and designated it the L 600. For the

Tiger B, Henschel used a modified version of the L 600 and assigned it the designation L 801. Henschel went with the double-differential steering system because it felt that the other types of steering systems then available lacked the durability and strength to turn a vehicle as large and heavy as the Tiger E.

The Tiger B had an overlapping wheel arrangement consisting of large road wheels connected by high-strength torsion bars. While the overlapping road wheel configuration on the Tiger B was an improvement over the interleaved road wheel arrangement of the Tiger E, overlapping road wheels place a potentially damaging twisting load on tank tracks and typically shorten their life span.

Design Dead Ends

Another heavy tank that was considered by the German army was named the *Maus* (Mouse). Hitler had ordered Porsche to begin design studies in June 1942 on a vehicle that was classified as a 'super-heavy tank'. It was anticipated that it would weigh approximately 314,000lb and be armed with a 128mm main gun and a coaxial 75mm gun, plus machine guns.

An order for 150 units of the *Maus* was cancelled in late 1943 by the German army. Only two half-completed prototypes were ever built, with another nine under construction when the war in Europe ended. From the March 1946 issue of a US army publication titled *Intelligence Bulletin* appears this passage from an article on the *Maus*:

> The Mouse is an amazing vehicle, with spectacular characteristics. The glacis plate up front is approximately 8 inches (200mm) thick. Since it is sloped at 35 degrees to the vertical, the armor basis is therefore 14 inches (356mm). Side armor is 7 inches (180mm) thick, with the rear protected by plates 6.25 inches (160mm) thick. The front of the turret is protected by 9.5 inches (240mm) of cast armor, while the 8-inch (200mm) thick turret sides and rear were sloped so as to give the effect of 9 inches (230mm) of armor.

The *Maus* was not the only super-heavy tank under development in late-war Germany. Another was designated the E-100. Development began in June 1943 by Krupp and it was originally envisioned that it was to be armed with the same weapon array as the *Maus*. The following year Hitler ordered all work on super-heavy tanks to be halted and only a single turretless prototype example of the E-100 was completed.

A US army report dated May 1945 had this to say about the E-100 prototype chassis located at the end of the war in Europe:

> A tank estimated to weigh approximately one hundred and ten tons ... that its external features resemble the Tiger B tank, with the following new features: (1) increased length and width, (2) heavier armor plate throughout, (3) wider track, (4) new suspension. The torsion bar is not used ... (5) spaced armor plate,

made in three sections is bolted to the side plates of the tank, giving a rounded surface at the sponsons … Major items lacking for the complete assembly are the gun, turret ring, suspension springs and drive sprockets.

The E-100 super-heavy tank was to have been the first in a series of new armoured fighting vehicles of varying sizes, weights, and assigned roles to be built by those German automotive firms not already involved in the design and production of tanks.

Italian Heavy Tanks

The Italian army had first begun considering a requirement for a heavy tank in 1938 that would not weigh more than approximately 45,000lb. For numerous technical reasons and ever-changing requirements, production of the heavy tank referred to as the P40, which weighed approximately 56,000lb, did not begin until the summer of 1943. It had a four-man crew and was armed with a 75mm main gun.

Only three complete units of the P40 and a number of incomplete examples were built before the Italian surrender in September 1943. The Germans kept the P40 factory open after the Italian surrender and forty examples in running order were constructed. These vehicles were employed by German military units engaged in anti-partisan duties. Approximately sixty engineless units of the P40 were deployed by the German army as defensive pillboxes in Italy.

There was some thought by the Italian army of ordering an up-armoured version of the P40 heavy tank labelled the 'P43 bis'. It was hoped that it would be comparable to the German Panther tank and armed with either a 75mm or 105mm main gun. The Italian surrender brought its development to an end and only a wooden mock-up was ever completed.

Hungarian Heavy Tanks

As the 40mm main gun on the Turan I medium tank was not able to fire an effective HE round, a progressively-improved version of the tank with a larger turret was armed with a 75mm gun. Reflecting the tank's up-arming and weight gain, it was labelled the Turan II heavy tank. Out of an original order for 332 units, only 139 were completed when production was terminated in 1944.

The last version of the Turan medium tank series proposed for service with the Hungarian army was labelled the Turan III heavy tank. It was fitted with a newly-designed turret armed with a version of a German 75mm tank gun designated the KwK 40 L/43. As the German government agreed to sell Panzer IV medium tanks to the Hungarian government in 1944, all work on the Turan III heavy tank came to an end and only a single prototype was built.

There was also some development work done on a Hungarian version of the Panther tank referred to as the *Tas* tank. In Hungarian army service it would have been considered a heavy tank. However, like the Turan III heavy tank, only a single prototype was built. That prototype was destroyed in an American bomber attack on the factory where it was located in July 1944. The only heavy tanks that were employed by the Hungarian army during the Second World War were ten units of the Tiger E supplied in 1944.

The Porsche-designed contender chassis for the German army's heavy tank competition is pictured with its Krupp-designed turret. It was labelled the VK 45.01(P) and had a hybrid (gasoline/electric) power plant. Testing showed that this cutting-edge technology had not yet been perfected, which made it very unreliable and therefore unacceptable to the German army. (*Patton Museum*)

Henschel's chief designer decided to stick with tried and proven technology with their heavy tank chassis submission. This decision led to them being awarded the contract. This illustration shows a Henschel pre-production Tiger E. It can be identified by a number of design features. These include no rear turret loader's hatch, no smoke grenade-launchers and no fenders. *(George Bradford)*

Pz Kpfw 'TIGER I' Ausf. E (initial prototypes)

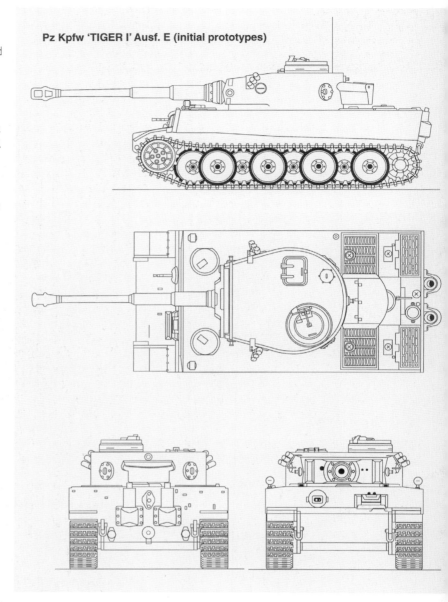

(**Opposite, above**) Tiger E tanks on the Henschel production line. The factory where the tanks were built employed 8,000 workers divided between two twelve-hour shifts. The uncompleted hulls and turrets were not built by Henschel but were delivered by other firms for them to assemble and complete. The tank hull on the right is having twin vertical boring machines drill out the turret ring. *(Patton Museum)*

(**Opposite, below**) At the Henschel factory we see the complicated interleaved road wheel arrangement on an early-production Tiger E tank. The original design of the tank consisted of forty-eight road wheels with twenty-four on either side of the hull connected by torsion bars. Tiger E tanks built after February 1944 had only thirty-two road wheels with sixteen on either side of the hull. *(Patton Museum)*

(**Above**) The chassis of a Tiger E tank being restored at a British museum. The front superstructure hatch openings were only for vehicle ingress and egress by the driver and radioman. Note that the rear hull engine compartment is divided into three sections, with the engine located in the centre. (*Tank Museum*)

(**Opposite page**) Being installed in a Tiger E at the Henschel factory is the vehicle's approximately 2,800lb Maybach liquid-cooled gasoline engine. The first 250 production units of the Tiger E had a 650hp engine labelled the HL210 P45 that proved unreliable in service. This was blamed on the fact that the engine had been rushed into production without sufficient testing. (*Patton Museum*)

(**Opposite, above**) In this photograph we see the front hull-mounted steering unit and box-like transmission being pulled from a Tiger E. The tank came with a double-differential steering system designated the L600. The transmission on the Tiger E was hydraulically-operated, semi-automatic and labelled the Olvar 40 12 16. (*Tank Museum*)

(**Opposite, below**) The final stage of production of the Tiger E at the Henschel factory is shown here with the turret being mated to its hull. Design features that identify this vehicle as an early-production example include the twin front headlights and the three-round grenade-launcher seen on either side of the vehicle's turret. This vehicle has the narrow railroad transport tracks fitted. (*Patton Museum*)

(**Above**) Taking part in a historical military event is a Tiger E belonging to a British museum. The rubber-rimmed road wheels and the drum-style vehicle commander's cupola were seen on the early and many of the mid-production Tiger E tanks built. The cupola had five vision slots protected by laminated ballistic glass arrayed around its circumference. (*Tank Museum*)

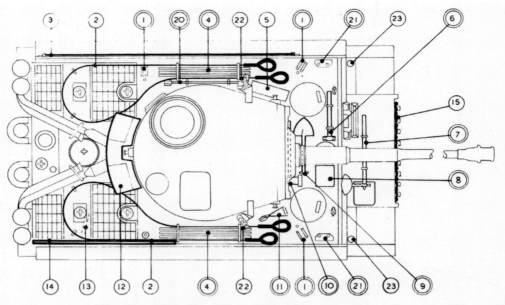

EXTERNAL STOWAGE. PzKw VI.H. Tiger.

KEY TO DIAGRAM

1: ANTI-PERSONNEL MINE ATTACHMENTS.
2: TOW ROPE.
3: 15 WIRE ROPE.
4: GUN CLEANING RODS.
5: BLANKING OFF PLATE FOR AIRSLIT ENGINE COMP'T.
6: SLEDGE HAMMER.

7: SHOVEL.
8: JACKING BLOCK.
9: SPADE.
10: AXE.
11: WIRE CUTTERS.
12: TURRET BIN (10 TRACK LINKS, 10 TRACK PINS)
13: TETRA FIRE EXTINGUISHER.

14: WIRELESS AERIAL STOWAGE.
15: SPARE TRACK LINKS.
20: CROW BAR 5'10"
21: HEAD LAMP POSITIONS.
22: SMOKE GENERATOR DISCHARERS.
23: HOLE FOR POLE SUPPORTING CAMOUFLAGE (CAMOUFLAGED AS LORRY OR BUS)

(**Above**) From a British army wartime technical evaluation report on a captured Tiger E from North Africa is this illustration. As with most tanks during their production runs, some of the external components noted here were changed or moved to different locations in response to factory modifications carried out based on user feedback. Some were done in the field by Tiger tank units. (*Tank Museum*)

(**Opposite, above**) In this ghosted illustration from a British army wartime report we see the many interior components of an early-production Tiger E labelled. Because the Tiger E transmission was semi-automatic the driver did not have to perform any manual clutching when switching between gears. Clutching was only required when starting the vehicle and between the forward and reverse gears. (*Tank Museum*)

(**Opposite, below**) With the turret from a Tiger E tank suspended in the air at a British museum a number of features are visible. The most noticeable is the canvas sack attached to the bottom rear of the recoil guard. It was there to catch spent main gun cartridge cases. The stanchion sloping down under the main gun supports the gunner's seat on the opposite side of the main gun. (*Tank Museum*)

MOUNTING FOR SCISSORS
TELESCOPE
WIRELESS
AERIAL
ESCAPE
HATCH
EXTRACTOR
FAN
TURRET
FUSE BOX
MOUNTING FOR RANGEFINDER
(STOWED POSITION)
HOLDER FOR BOX
CONTAINING M.G.
GROUND MOUNTING
FOR
WATER BOTTLE
BINOCULAR
TELESCOPE
BALANCE
SPRING
CYLINDER
SMOKE GENERATOR
DISCHARGERS
SPARE GLASS
BLOCKS
COMMANDER'S SEAT
TRAVERSE HANDWHEEL
(Commander)
CLINOMETER
REVOLVER
PORT
8.8 CM.
AMMUNITION BINS
M.G.
ACCESSORIES
8.8 CM.
AMMN. BINS
TRAVERSE
HANDWHEEL (Gunner)
COMMANDER'S
SHIELD
TRAVERSE
GEARBOX
PETROL
TANK
PETROL
PRIMER
M.G. AMMUNITION
FAN DRIVE
CLUTCH LEVER
AIR INTAKE
VALVE CONTROL
PETROL TAP
MOUNTING FOR
WIRELESS SET
C. BRAKE
DRUM
8.8 CM.
AMMN.
UNDER FLOOR
ELEVATING
HANDWHEEL
(Gunner)
GUN FIRING
LEVER
SHOCK
ABSORBER
STEERING
UNIT
STEERING
WHEEL
GUNNER'S
SEAT
VENTILATION
CONTROL
GEAR
SELECTOR
CONTROL
LEVER
DIRECTION
CONTROL
LEVER
GEARBOX
FWD & BACK
AMMN.
M.G. FIRING
PEDAL
HYDRAULIC
TRAVERSE UNIT
DRIVER'S
SEAT
STARTER
CARB. Q.
CONTROLS
HAND
BRAKE
FIRE
EXTINGUISHER
HYDRAULIC TRAVERSE
FOOT CONTROL
PETROL
TANK
EMERGENCY
STEERING
LEVERS
SHOCK
ABSORBER
8.8 CM.
AMMUNITION BINS
TORSION BAR
SUSPENSION
ACCELERATOR
FOOT
BRAKE
CLUTCH

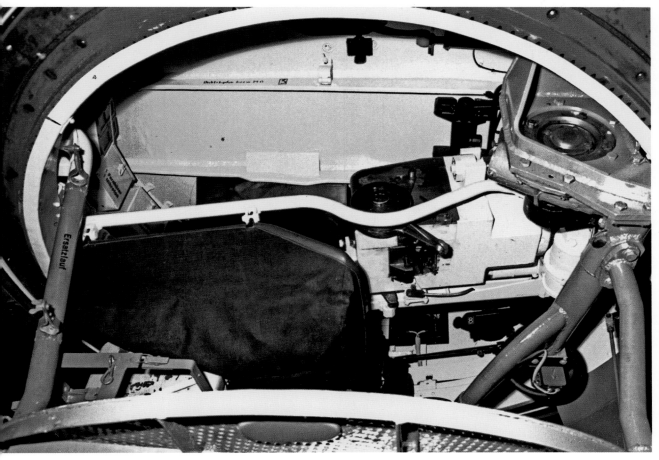

Ersatzlauf

Dichtkopfen form M.6

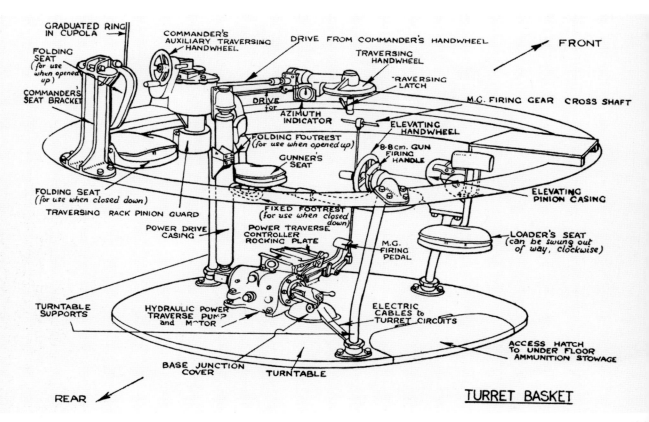

GRADUATED RING IN CUPOLA

COMMANDER'S AUXILIARY TRAVERSING HANDWHEEL

DRIVE FROM COMMANDER'S HANDWHEEL

FRONT

FOLDING SEAT (for use when opened up)

TRAVERSING HANDWHEEL

COMMANDERS SEAT BRACKET

TRAVERSING LATCH

DRIVE for AZIMUTH INDICATOR

M.G. FIRING GEAR CROSS SHAFT

ELEVATING HANDWHEEL

FOLDING FOOTREST (for use when opened up)

8·8 cm. GUN FIRING HANDLE

GUNNERS SEAT

FOLDING SEAT (for use when closed down)

ELEVATING PINION CASING

TRAVERSING RACK PINION GUARD

FIXED FOOTREST (for use when closed down)

POWER DRIVE CASING

POWER TRAVERSE CONTROLLER ROCKING PLATE

M.G. FIRING PEDAL

LOADER'S SEAT (can be swung out of way, clockwise)

TURNTABLE SUPPORTS

HYDRAULIC POWER TRAVERSE PUMP and MOTOR

ELECTRIC CABLES to TURRET CIRCUITS

ACCESS HATCH TO UNDER FLOOR AMMUNITION STOWAGE

BASE JUNCTION COVER

TURNTABLE

REAR

TURRET BASKET

(**Opposite, above**) From a British army wartime report appears this illustration of the turret basket on a Tiger E. The floor of the turret basket attached to the tank's turret ring at different points and rotated with the turret. On the floor of the turret basket is the labelled power traverse rocking plate employed by the gunner to traverse the turret. (*Tank Museum*)

(**Above**) In this picture of a Tiger E tank we see the various interior components of the main gun. The two hooks hanging from the ceiling are part of the internal travel lock for the main gun. They held the main gun steady when not in use and took the inertia load off the elevating gearbox. Also visible are the two turret pistol ports: one inside the turret and the other on the exterior. (*Andreas Kirchhoff*)

(**Opposite, below**) In this photo taken inside a Tiger E we see the loader's fold-up seat. To the left of the loader's seat is the breech of the main gun with the two overhead hooks being the internal travel lock for the weapon. Also visible is the canvas bag attached to the bottom of the recoil guard that held spent main gun cartridge cases. (*Tank Museum*)

In front of and to the left of the vehicle commander's lower seat position in this Tiger E is the metal housing for the vehicle commander's auxiliary traversing hand wheel. By folding out his vertical seat backrest into a horizontal position, the vehicle commander could sit on it, open his overhead hatch and look out over the top of the cupola. (*Tank Museum*)

(**Opposite, above**) The gunner's articulated binocular sight is seen here in this Tiger E. It was designated the TZF 9b and had a 2.5 power magnification. Beginning in March 1944, all new production Tiger E tanks were fitted with an articulated monocular sight labelled the TZF 9c. It provided the gunner with both a 2.5 and 5 power magnification. (*Tank Museum*)

(**Opposite, below**) Inside the turret of a Tiger E we see the gunner's seat cushion. Below the seat we can see the powered rocker plates for traversing the turret. To the right of the vehicle commander's seat is a sheet metal guard that divided the space between the vehicle commander and loader. It was there to protect the vehicle commander from any flashback when the breech block opened upon recoil. (*Tank Museum*)

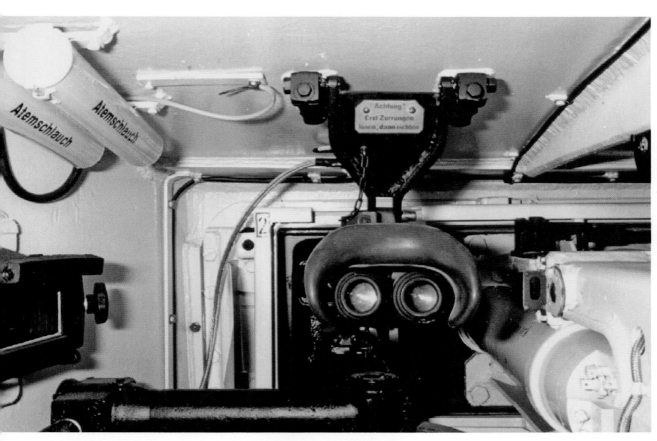

(**Opposite, page**) From the loader's position on a Tiger E looking forward the mounting bracket for the coaxial machine gun is visible. However, the coaxial machine gun is not fitted in this vehicle. When fitted the coaxial 7.92mm machine gun was fired mechanically by a foot pedal operated by the gunner. The cylinder to the left of the machine-gun mounting bracket is for the pneumatically-operated counter-recoil buffer (shock absorber). (*Tank Museum*)

(**Above**) A loader on a Tiger E is shown clutching an armour-piercing (AP) shell. The loaders had a direct vision port in the right-hand side turret wall protected by laminated ballistic glass. Beginning in March 1943, all new production Tiger E tanks came off the assembly line with a fixed periscope in the turret roof for the loader. (*Patton Museum*)

This wartime illustration shows the main gun ammunition storage arrangement in a Tiger E tank. There was authorized storage space in the vehicle for ninety-two main gun rounds. Thirty-two were stored horizontally in racks with fold-down doors on either side of the superstructure. Six were located to the left of the driver with the remainder stored horizontally on the hull floor in metal boxes. (*National Archives*)

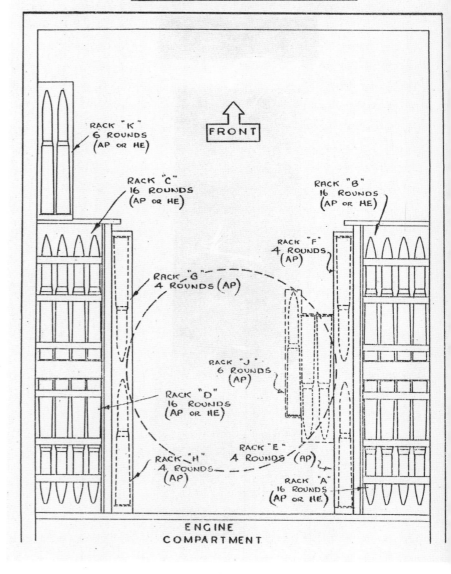

– TIGER –
PLAN OF AMMUNITION STOWAGE

FRONT

RACK "K"
6 ROUNDS
(AP OR HE)

RACK "C"
16 ROUNDS
(AP OR HE)

RACK "B"
16 ROUNDS
(AP OR HE)

RACK "F"
4 ROUNDS
(AP)

RACK "G"
4 ROUNDS (AP)

RACK "J"
6 ROUNDS
(AP)

RACK "D"
16 ROUNDS
(AP OR HE)

RACK "E"
4 ROUNDS (AP)

RACK "H"
4 ROUNDS
(AP)

RACK "A"
16 ROUNDS
(AP OR HE)

ENGINE
COMPARTMENT

(**Opposite, above**) One of the large sixteen-round superstructure side main gun ammunition storage bins is seen in this picture taken inside a Tiger E. The box in front of and below the sixteen-round bin has room for four rounds. One German Tiger E crewman informed his British captors that his vehicle had been modified to carry as many as 120 main gun rounds. (*Frank Schulz*)

(**Opposite, below**) In this picture we see the loader's escape hatch on a Tiger E. Like the rear turret wall loader's hatch on the Panther tank series, it could be utilized by the loader to discard spent main gun cartridge cases when opened. Because the hatch was not spring-assisted it could only be closed from the outside when opened. (*Tank Museum*)

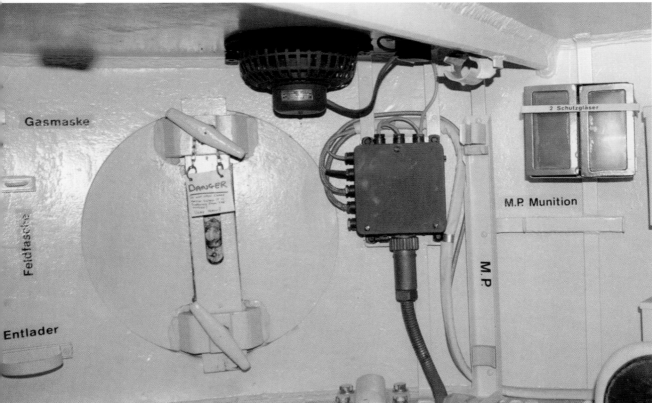

Gasmaske

Feldtasche

Entlader

DANGER

2 Schutzglaser

M.P. Munition

M.P.

The radioman's position is seen in this picture of an unrestored Tiger E tank. Visible is the mounting bracket for the machine gun. To the left of the radioman's position, his seat and backrest are missing from this vehicle, as is the transmission housing upon which his AM radio communication gear was affixed. The antenna for the radio was located on the right rear of the tank's superstructure. *(Andreas Kirchhoff)*

(**Opposite, above**) Somewhere on the Eastern Front an early-production Tiger E with rubber-rimmed road wheels is being loaded with main gun rounds. On the left of the tanker standing on the superstructure is the closed loader's escape hatch. The large bins on the rear of the turret were for storing extra track links and track pins to hold the tracks together. *(Patton Museum)*

(**Opposite, below**) The armour visor arrangement on a Tiger E is pictured here. Combat experience showed that the laminated ballistic vision blocks were easily damaged by small-arms fire and sometimes became jammed in place. Late-production Tiger E tanks lacked the two small aperture openings directly above the driver's armour visor for a binocular sight. On this particular vehicle they have been plugged. *(Tank Museum)*

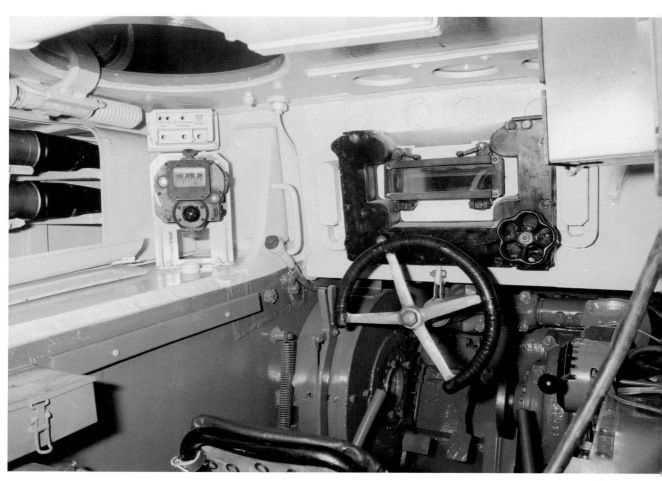

(**Opposite, above**) In this picture of the driver's position on a Tiger E tank we can see an electrically-operated gyroscopic direction indicator (compass) to his left. The driver's seat was adjustable for forward and backward movement but could not be raised or lowered. This was not necessary as the driver's overhead hatch was not directly over his seat, as is obvious in this photograph. (*Tank Museum*)

(**Opposite, below**) The dramatic difference in size between the Tiger E and the Panzer III series medium tank is well-illustrated in this photograph. The Tiger E's massive service tracks were of cast-manganese construction, 28.5in in width and consisted of ninety-six track links held together by unlubricated removable steel pins. With the service tracks fitted the tank had a width of 12ft 3in. (*Tank Museum*)

(**Above**) Beginning in July 1943, Tiger E tanks coming off the assembly lines were fitted with the new low-profile cast-armour vehicle commander's cupola pictured here. It had seven hooded periscopes arrayed around its circumference. The attachment rail around the top of the cupola is for the mounting of a machine gun intended for anti-aircraft protection. (*Frank Schulz*)

(**Above**) A major external design change eventually applied to the Tiger E tank production line was the replacement of the original forty-eight inverted, dish-like rubber-rimmed road wheels. In their place appeared thirty-two flat steel road wheels (sixteen on either side of the hull) as seen on this preserved late-production Tiger E tank in Western Europe. The rubber was now inside the steel road wheels. (*Ian Wilcox*)

(**Opposite, above**) On display at a British museum is one of three pre-production examples of the Tiger B tank. This particular example has one of the turrets designed by Porsche and built by Krupp for the rejected Porsche version of the Tiger B. The vehicle was found at a German army testing facility at the end of the war in Europe and shipped back to Great Britain for technical evaluation. (*Tank Museum*)

(**Opposite, below**) In an obviously staged wartime photograph British army soldiers are shown examining a knocked-out Tiger B tank. It is fitted with one of the Porsche-designed turrets built by Krupp. The fact that the large and heavy turret is ajar indicates that an internal explosion occurred due to the onboard main gun ammunition being detonated. (*Tank Museum*)

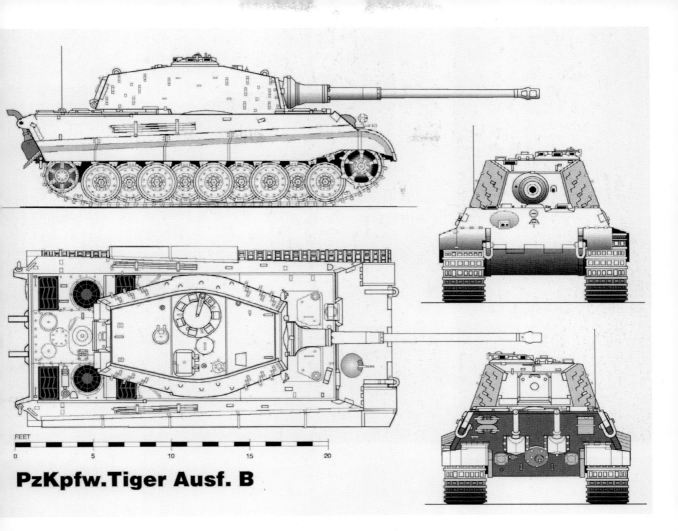

FEET

0   5   10   15   20

PzKpfw. Tiger Ausf. B

(**Opposite, above**) A Tiger B with a Porsche turret is seen here on a French road. Note the one-piece tapered superstructure plate similar to that fitted to the Panther Ausf. G. It has two aperture holes in the front of the turret for the gunner's articulated binocular sight. An articulated monocular sight began appearing on the Tiger B production line in April 1944. (*Tank Museum*)

(**Opposite, below**) The curved front turret plate on the Tiger B pictured marks it as one of the Porsche turrets modified for fitting on the Henschel chassis. The curved turret gun shield of the Porsche design unintentionally created a shot trap also known as a re-entrant angle. Note the steel-rimmed flat road wheels that also appeared on late-production Tiger E tanks. (*Tank Museum*)

(**Above**) In this line illustration we see the various design features of a Henschel chassis fitted with the series production turret. On the roof of the vehicle, between the vehicle commander's cupola and the loader's overhead hatch, is the circular upper portion of the electrically-powered turret exhaust fan. To the lower right of the fan is the small opening for the close-defence breech-loading mortar inside the turret. (*George Bradford*)

(**Opposite, above**) This preserved example of a Tiger B on display in Western Europe is fitted with the series production turret designed and produced by Krupp for the winning Henschel heavy tank chassis. It was cheaper, easier to build and did away with the shot trap/re-entrant angle on the Porsche turrets, which had resulted in some projectiles being deflected downward into the hull. (*Andreas Kirchhoff*)

(**Opposite, below**) In this photograph we can see the escape hatch in the rear turret plate of this preserved Tiger B with the series production turret. As with the Panther tank series, the Tiger E and Tiger B turret traverse rates were governed by their engine speed. At the maximum engine rpm the Tiger B turret could be rotated 360 degrees in nineteen seconds. (*Ian Wilcox*)

(**Above**) Belonging to the collection of a German army museum is this restored Tiger B with the series production turret. In front of the tank are two main gun rounds. On the left is a high-explosive (HE) round with an adjustable fuze on its nose. To its right is an armour-piercing (AP) round. The cartridge cases for the main gun rounds for the 88mm main gun on the Tiger B were almost double the size of those for the 88mm main gun on the Tiger E. (*Frank Schulz*)

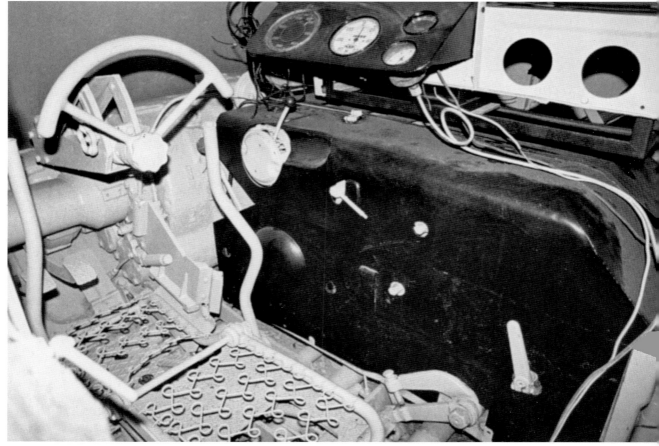

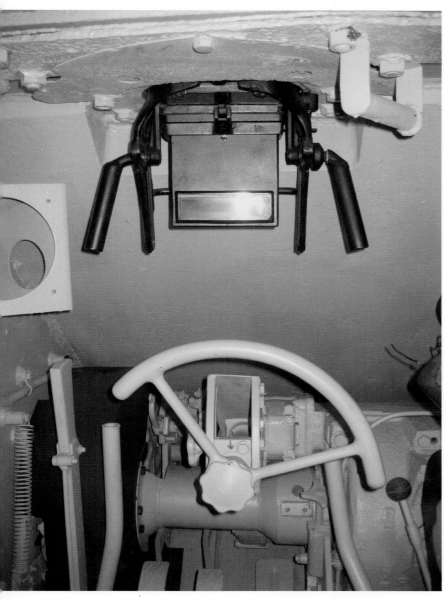

Looking upward from the driver's seat on a Tiger B is the interior portion of his 360-degree rotating and tilting overhead periscope. The same periscope was fitted to the Panther Ausf. G driver's position. This reflected German industry's late-war efforts to rationalize production by sharing as many components between tanks as possible to cut costs and speed up their production times. (*Author's collection*)

(**Opposite, above**) On display during a historical military vehicle event held by a British museum is a restored Tiger B. The overlapping road wheel arrangement of the Tiger B or the interleaved road wheel arrangement of its predecessor were never copied on any post-war tank designs. This is because they were too heavy and more difficult to maintain in the field than anticipated. (*David Marian*)

(**Opposite, below**) Pictured is the driver's position on a Tiger B tank and the large transmission housing upon which his instrument panel is fitted. Also seen in this photograph is the shift control unit for the driver and the two back-up steering levels on either side of his seat. With the tank's transmission in neutral the driver of the Tiger E and Tiger B could perform a 360-degree pivot or neutral steer. (*Author's collection*)

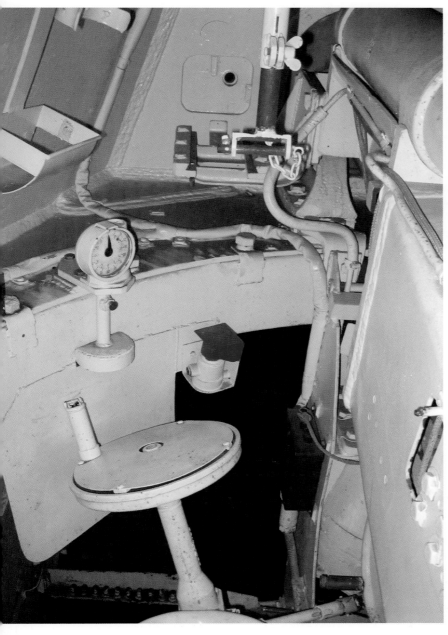

From the gunner's position on a Tiger B looking forward at the upper portion of this image can be seen the mounted attachment points for the articulated monocular gun sight not present in this vehicle. In the bottom portion of the picture is the gunner's manually-operated traversing hand wheel for the tank's turret. To his left is his twelve-hour azimuth (direction) indicator. (*Author's collection*)

(**Opposite, above**) The rounded gun cast-armour shield on this restored Tiger B fitted with a series production turret is known in the German language as a *Saukopfblende*. It is approximately 175mm at its thickest point. The *Zimmerit* anti-magnetic mine paste on the tank seen had been applied to all production units at the factory until ordered to be discontinued on all German tanks in September 1944. (*Ken Estes*)

(**Opposite, below**) American soldiers are looking at the larger of two penetration points on this Tiger B fitted with the series production turret. There were two types of main gun barrels fitted to the Tiger B, with the majority being the two-piece version seen here. The two-piece barrel began appearing on the Tiger B production line in April 1944. Those built before then were fitted with a single-piece (monobloc) barrel. (*Patton Museum*)

Shown is the breech end of the 88mm main gun on a Tiger B. On the top of the breech housing are the two long cylinders that comprise part of the main gun's recoil system. The cylinder on the left of the picture is the hydro-pneumatic recuperator. Its job is to store the main gun recoil energy that will be needed to return the main gun barrel to its original firing position following the recoil movement. (*Author's collection*)

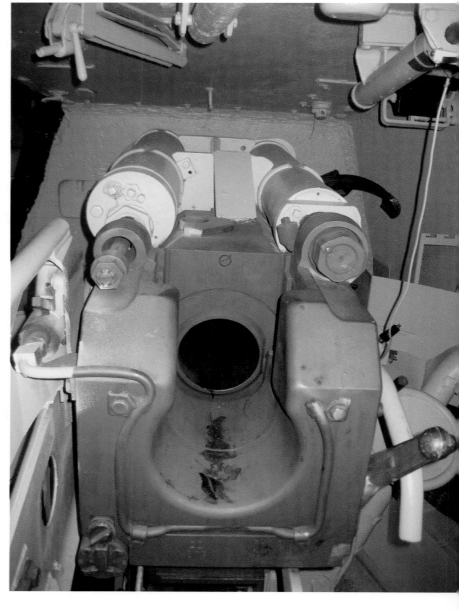

(**Opposite, above**) Seen here on display at the now-closed Patton Museum of Armor and Cavalry is a Tiger B with the series production turret. The cut-away turret and superstructure feature of this particular vehicle allows the viewer to see the mannequins dressed in period uniforms at the vehicle commander and gunner's positions. (*Author's collection*)

(**Opposite, below**) Looking down into the turret of a Tiger B we can see the loader's fold-up seat and his manually-operated turret traverse hand wheel. On the bottom of the turret basket floor is the hydraulically-operated turret traversing pump and motor. Upon testing captured Tiger B tanks, the British army concluded that the loader's position was far superior to that on the Tiger E due to there being more room. (*Author's collection*)

From a wartime British army report appears this illustration of the main gun ammunition storage arrangement on a Tiger B with the series production turret. There was horizontal storage in the superstructure for sixty-four main gun rounds and another twenty-two in the rear turret bustle. In the American and British armies the rear turret bustle main gun rounds were referred to as 'ready rounds'. (*Tank Museum*)

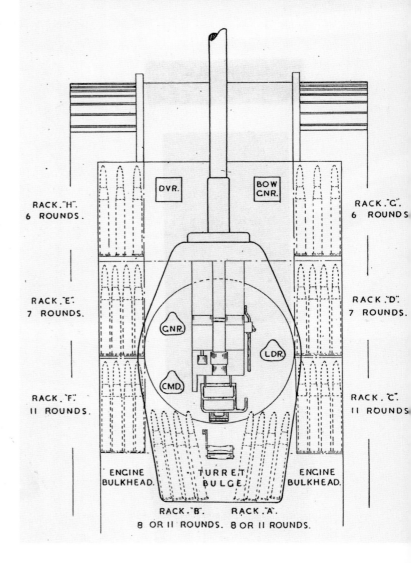

ROYAL TIGER.

PLAN OF AMMUNITION STOWAGE.

RACK."H". 6 ROUNDS.

DVR.

BOW CNR.

RACK."G". 6 ROUNDS

RACK."E". 7 ROUNDS.

GNR.

LDR.

RACK."D". 7 ROUNDS.

RACK."F". II ROUNDS.

CMD.

RACK."C". II ROUNDS

ENGINE BULKHEAD.

TURRET BULGE.

ENGINE BULKHEAD.

RACK."B". 8 OR II ROUNDS.

RACK."A". 8 OR II ROUNDS.

(**Opposite, above**) This photo taken from the commander's seat on a Tiger B shows the rear turret bustle. Visible at the very rear of the turret bustle is a hatch. This could be employed as an escape hatch or a pathway for main gun rounds to be passed to the loader inside the turret. Note the vertical roller that was there to help ease the loader's job with the large and heavy main gun rounds. (*Author's collection*)

(**Opposite, below**) Looking up from the loader's position on a Tiger B tank one can see the complicated mechanism for his overhead hatch. To the left of the hatch is the bottom portion of the electrically-powered turret exhaust fan. Behind the loader's hatch can be seen the incomplete bottom portion of the close-defence weapon breech. To the left of the close-defence weapon breech and in the far background of this picture can be seen the bottom portion of the loader's overhead fixed periscope. (*Author's collection*)

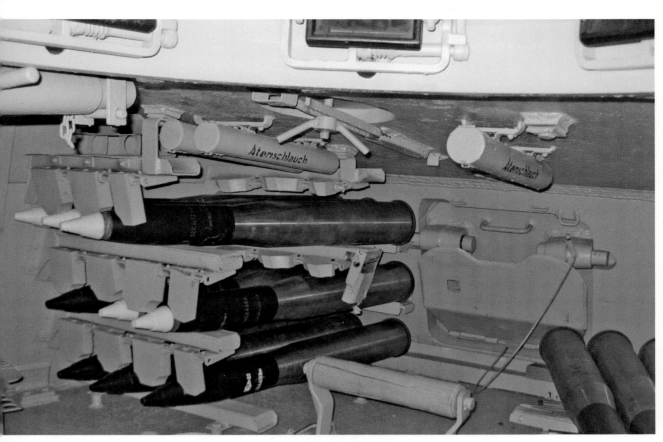

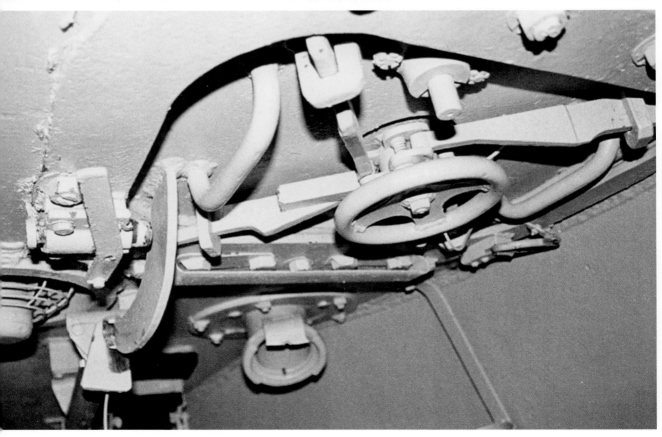

From the front of a Tiger B turret we can see both the gunner's hand wheel for manually traversing the vehicle's turret and behind and above that feature the seat and backrest for the vehicle commander. Both the gunner and vehicle commander's seat bottoms and backrests fold to one side when not required. *(Author's collection)*

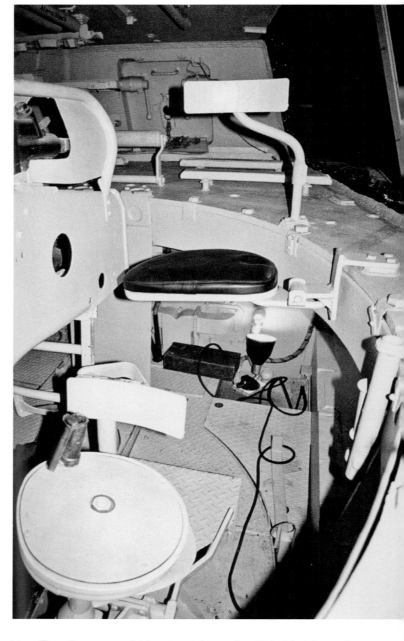

(**Opposite, above**) In this picture taken inside a Tiger B we see a fold-out metal tray directly behind the main gun breech. When a spent main gun cartridge case ejected from the breech during the main gun recoil cycle it struck the deflector plate seen at the rear of the tray. At that point the loader picked up the cartridge case and hurled it out of the tank through an opening in the turret roof. *(Author's collection)*

(**Opposite, below**) On the turret roof of this Tiger B we can see a number of design features. On the left of the image is the vehicle commander's cupola and on the right the loader's overhead hatch. In the middle foreground is the closed overhead hatch for the loader to dispose of spent main gun cartridge cases. In the middle background is the upper portion of the turret exhaust fan. *(Frank Schulz)*

(**Opposite, above**) A close-up of the ball machine-gun mount in the front glacis of a Tiger B. The only US army vehicle in Western Europe that stood a chance of knocking out a Tiger B at normal combat ranges was the M36 tank destroyer armed with the 90mm gun M3 and the T-26 heavy tank armed with the same main gun. (*Patton Museum*)

(**Opposite, below**) A picture of a knocked-out Tiger B with what appears to be a large-bore penetration through its right side turret wall. The turret and superstructure/lower hull of the Tiger B was constructed of rolled homogenous armour (RHA) plates. To strengthen them the RHA plates were joined together by overlapped stepped welded joints dovetailed together. (*Patton Museum*)

(**Above**) On this restored Tiger B belonging to a Swiss museum we can see the dovetailed joint connecting the rolled homogenous armour (RHA) glacis with the lower front hull RHA armour plate. RHA has always offered a higher level of protection when struck by large-calibre armour-piercing (AP) projectiles than cast homogenous armour (CHA) or face-hardened armour due to its ductility. (*Pierre-Olivier Buan*)

(**Opposite, above**) A Tiger B resides in a farmer's field either due to battle damage or mechanical problems of some sort. The biggest disadvantage with rolled homogenous armour (RHA) plates is their inability to be formed into complex shapes. Hence the use of cast homogenous armour (CHA) for the tank's gun shield seen in this picture as well as the vehicle commander's cupola. (*Tank Museum*)

(**Above**) On display in France as a monument vehicle is this preserved and well-kept French army Char B1 bis heavy tank. It was armed with a turret-mounted 47mm gun and a 75mm gun/howitzer in the front hull with limited traverse. In German army service it was labelled the Panzer B2 740(f) and employed in a variety of roles. (*Pierre-Olivier Buan*)

(**Opposite, below**) In January 1943, Dr Ferdinand Porsche had been tasked by Hitler to begin design work on a heavy tank weighing 170 tons armed with two large-calibre guns. It was assigned the name *Maus* (Mouse). One of the two prototypes is seen here during testing. The project was cancelled in November 1944 by the German army. (*Patton Museum*)

(**Opposite, above**) Parked under a camouflage net is the single uncompleted prototype chassis of the built E-100 super-heavy tank discovered by the US army at the end of the war in Europe. No turret for the vehicle was ever built. It was the Krupp counterpart of the *Maus* but never progressed very far due to the very low priority assigned to it by the German army. (*Patton Museum*)

(**Opposite, below**) In October 1943, Hitler visited the German army's weapon-testing centre. For his inspection a number of full-scale wooden mock-ups of German-designed and built turretless tank destroyers were placed on display. For whatever reason, the test centre staff also decided to display this prototype of an Italian-designed and built heavy tank in the foreground labelled the P40. (*Patton Museum*)

(**Above**) One of two preserved Italian-designed and built P40 heavy tanks is shown here on display at an army base in Rome. None were completed in time to see service before the Italian surrender to the Western Allies in September 1943. Approximately 100 units were built under German supervision with more than half not having engines fitted. (*Pierre-Olivier Buan*)

This grainy photograph shows several examples of the Hungarian army 41M Turan II heavy tank armed with a short-barrelled, low-velocity 75mm main gun. In concept, the 41M Turan II was to act as a fire-support vehicle for the 41M Turan I medium tank armed with a 40mm main gun. This was akin to the original relationship envisioned for the German army Panzer III and Panzer IV medium tanks. (*Charles Kliment collection*)

Serving on the Eastern Front along with their German allies the Hungarian army 41M Turan II heavy tanks faced the same threat from Red Army 14.5mm anti-tank rifles. As a countermove they began applying to their heavy tanks the steel wire mesh spaced armour arrangement seen here. This feature had appeared on the German army Panzer IV Ausf. J beginning in September 1944. (*Charles Kliment collection*)

The final configuration of the Hungarian army Turan series was the Turan III heavy tank. In lieu of the short-barrelled, low-velocity 75mm main gun that armed its predecessor, the Turan III was armed with a long-barrelled, high-velocity 75mm main gun fitted with a muzzle brake. Only the single prototype of the vehicle seen here was built. *(Charles Kliment collection)*

Notes

Notes